The Illustrated Kemlows Story

THE ILLUSTRATED KEMLOWS STORY

(INCLUDING THE MASTERMODEL STORY)

Paul Brookes

Copyright © Paul Brookes 2009

Published by Paul Brookes
2009

All rights reserved. No part of this publication may be reproduced or transmitted in any form or by any means, electronic or mechanical, including photocopy or any storage or retreival system without permission in writing from the publisher

ISBN 978 0 9561879 0 1

Designed and typeset by MRM Graphics Ltd
www.mrmgraphics.co.uk

Printed and bound by Kyodo Nation Printing in Thailand, under the supervision of MRM Graphics Ltd, Winslow, Bucks

CONTENTS

Acknowledgements		vii
Preface		viii
Introduction		ix
Chapter One	Company Development	1
Chapter Two	Early Products	11
Chapter Three	The BJ Ward Influence	29
Chapter Four	The MasterModel Range	35
Chapter Five	MasterModel Derivatives	125
Chapter Six	Kemlows K-Series	131
Chapter Seven	Other Kemlows diecast Products	155
Chapter Eight	Kemlows Plastics	167
Appendices		177
Bibliography		178

To Leanne and Laura

ACKNOWLEDGEMENTS

This book would not have got off the ground without the initial enthusiasm and hard work of Jennifer who deciphered notes and compiled Kemlows ledger databases. To her, a great thanks.

Stephen Lowe, the son of William Lowe (a founder member of Kemlows) who with his wife Brenda have provided me with the type of information and anecdotes only available from 'the inside'.

Pat Hammond who, all those years ago, initiated Jennifer and myself into writing down all we knew about our particular toy interest. The MasterModel Gallery in Model Railway Enthusiast got it all going.

Bob Smith who ploughed through the draft and made helpful comments and observations.

Last, but not least, Martin Rose who before going off to University took all this from my own scrawl, corrected all the grammatical errors and got it onto a computer linked with all the pictures.

PREFACE

As a model railway historian, I have become very critical of the way the history of a company has been recorded. Histories of this kind need to be two things – on the one hand they need to be enjoyable and interesting to read and on the other hand they need to be the ultimate reference book, with information that is both comprehensive and easy to find. It takes a very special writer to achieve both of these and in Paul Brookes we have found such a person.

I have known Paul for many years, in fact, since he first turned up at my stall at a York Racecourse swapmeet wearing a huge badge that declared he was looking for MasterModels. As a former collector of the range, I soon got talking to him and we have been talking about MasterModels, and many others of the less well known model railway accessory brands, ever since. Over the years it has been obvious that Paul is a real enthusiast who enjoys the hunt for the origins of his subject and each time we meet I enjoy listening to his most recent adventures. His keen search for history comes through in this book which contains many anecdotes that his research has uncovered.

We have here a groundbreaking and definitive book, which is beautifully illustrated and will survive as the standard work on Kemlows. Enjoy it!

Pat Hammond

INTRODUCTION

Jennifer's and my own interest in MasterModels started in 1990 when Jennifer and I first met. Trying to impress Jennifer, I took her one Sunday morning to a John Webb toy fair at Mansfield Leisure Centre. With hindsight this was a very expensive move. My aim was to add items to my Hornby Dublo collection. By chance Jennifer saw some mint boxed MasterModels on Rolande Allen's table.

"Now these are nice," she exclaimed. We ended up buying most of what Rolande had. The boxed 'AA' set springs to mind. Over the following years the Hornby Dublo has given way to MasterModels and our keenness in researching these items developed.

In 1998 we were asked by Pat Hammond, then Editor of Model Railway Enthusiast to present a feature on MasterModels. The MasterModel Gallery ran from June 1998 until March 2001 with items in every month.

In August 1998 we published 'Listings of Models for Collectors' in which we itemised every MasterModel known, with a description. Since then there has been a call for a comprehensive colour reference book.

We were diverted a little by our interest in other items related to the B J Ward stable, but after many meetings with Stephen Lowe (of Kemlows) the company history has been put together, with that of their production of MasterModels. Whilst MasterModels were a major part of the Kemlows output, other ranges were produced.

This has been a major project as nothing has been written on the complete Kemlows story before. What I have attempted to do is tell the Kemlows story in a historical context and list all items known to exist.

Of course, there may be some details still out there that have been missed. Any further information would be gladly received.

Paul Brookes April 2009

One

Company Development

William Arthur Lowe was a butcher by trade until he was called up for WWII. Whilst in the Services he met Charles Kempster, a butcher from Hackney.

After demob, there was meat rationing and so little or no work for butchers. Charlie Kempster and William Lowe both found work as navvies on demolition sites in London. Scrap lead was plentiful.

William married Lilian in 1944 and moved into 83 Westbury Ave, Turnpike Lane, Wood Green with William's parents.

As the friendship developed, Charlie met William's sister Nellie. William's wife Lilian tells the story of when Charlie came to tea with William, Nellie and herself. Charlie signalled to William (they had both been in the Signal Corps) that he had a fancy for Nellie. A relationship developed and they later married.

Just before they were married, Nellie lived at 37 Lansdowne Road, Wood Green in a third floor flat. The local rag and bone man, Reg Aldridge (Nellie's Uncle), gave Nellie a casting die he had come across on his rounds so that she could make lead soldiers to help finance her wedding dress.

Reg had used the die himself, but the fumes were now irritating his lung condition. After complaints about fumes from Nellie's neighbours, William and Lilian offered to help out. Minor production started in the upstairs kitchen at 83 Westbury Ave on a gas ring. The lead was scavenged off bomb sites and melted down in a saucepan. William and Charlie took over in the evening whilst Lilian and Nellie fettled and painted the soldiers. They were believed to be red and stitched onto red card. Charlie was tasked with trying to sell the soldiers to local toy shops. This was now about 1945.

83 Westbury Ave

At this time Kempster and Lowe met Ray Jackson who had previously worked nearby at DCMT (diecasting Machine Tools Ltd) and so had knowledge of the diecasting process.

Kemlows Diecasting Products was formed in 1946 with the directors: Charlie Kempster (as a family member and notionally in charge of marketing), William Lowe (business development - William turned out to be the driving force) and Ray Jackson (diecasting expertise).

David Lowe was born in 1946 and later became the Managing Director of Kemlows.

Jackson did not remain with the company long and went to the USA or Canada. He was bought out by William and Charlie for the same amount the he had originally invested.

With expansion production moved to the cellar at 60 St John's Street, Clerkenwell, North London. Only the cellar was rented and it became a bit of a sweat shop, but business prospered and Lilian's brother John Strange joined the family business

In 1947/8 as business prospered, a barn at the bottom of 83 Westbury Ave

Stephen Lowe with Mr Thurlow outside original buildings. 83 Westbury Ave, 2008

Original barn at 83 Westbury Ave 2008

Original barn at 83 Westbury Ave 2008

Downstairs in the barn was the foundry

Upstairs in the barn

became available for rent. This was converted into a foundry and outbuildings were erected for office and fettling etc.

In 1949, William's family moved out of 83 Westbury Ave to nearby Pellatt Grove. Stephen Lowe was born who later became a Technical Sales Director of the company. The factory continued production at 83 Westbury Ave.

Factory at Potters Bar, 1958

Factory 2008 (no longer Kemlows)

In 1958, business was good and still expanding. New products were continually being released. This resulted in a move from Westbury Ave to No 8 Station Road, Potters Bar.

An interesting note here. At the back of the factory was an M55 casting machine that pressure diecasted lead. In particular they made battery terminals. It is therefore quite possible that Kemlows produced a few cast lead items, even though there is no record. A lead Monet type bridge springs to Stephen Lowe's mind.

Next door but one to the new Kemlows factory was Collis Plastics. Collis Production were a plastic injection moulding firm and produced plastic components for Kemlows. For example Kemlows would make the diecast petrol pumps and Collis the plastic globes to go on them.

After Kemlows arrived at Potters Bar, Collis became involved in diecast toolmaking as well so as to supply Kemlows.

Collis were now producing tools for both Kemlows and themselves. It is possible the tool room made the diecast figures for the MasterModel range and

Collis site in 2008

so plastic ones as well. Randall (Merit) was a big customer of Kemlows and may have bought the plastic figures from Collis. According to Stephen Lowe this is perhaps the most plausible reason why some of the 'Merit' plastic figures are identical to Kemlows MasterModel diecast figures.

Because of the increased business with Collis, Kemlows bought Collis in 1972 from the owner Jeff Jeffries who was in bad health at that time.

This enabled Kemlows to move into the plastic business more efficiently, producing the Build-a-Garage Series of items and distributing through aB (Barton) and Barton's Motoplay. Collis was producing plastic items well into the 1970s. Stephen Lowe was in charge of the plastics division until William and Charlie split in 1976.

Next door to Kemlows at Potters Bar was Potters Bar Enamelling, which was owned by Kempster and Lowe and run by Charlie Ball and Reg Williams. Both were good friends of William Lowe and many items (and different paint jobs) were "cooked up" between them according to Stephen.

During the 1960s the MasterModels range had been running for 10 years and

The site of Potters Bar Enamelling in 2008 adjacent to the old Kemlows factory

other companies were emerging with plastic products: Merit, for example.

Kemlows other diecast products such as the Sentry Box Series and some Master Range Series were military vehicles. In the early 1960s Mary Whitehouse's campaign against military toys (she believed that playing aggressive and violent games resulted in children growing up with these tendencies) resulted in Woolworths withdrawing all their Kemlows items. This almost sent Kemlows to the wall. Nevertheless, business was good. Between the mid sixties and mid seventies, a secondary workshop was in operation on Billet Road, Walthamstow.

Whilst still making toys in the 1970s the new emphasis was on industrial castings and Kemlows slowly withdrew from toy manufacturing. In about 1978 Kemlows sold the tools and manufacturing rights to Barton Toys, but Collis and Kemlows carried on producing the respective parts for Barton's Motoplay until orders faded away in the 1980s.

It was in 1974 that Kemlows moved to their present premises at Hoddesdon, Hertfordshire. This factory was purpose built to Kemlows design.

COMPANY DEVELOPMENT

The newly purpose built Kemlows factory at Hoddesdon in 1974

In 1994 Kemlows put in place Strategic Business Planning with major investment. They had world class status using Cellular Teams and supplied pressure diecasting throughout the UK.

In 2001, Kemlows was sold by Stephen Lowe and his brother, David, to a management buyout.

Two

Early Products

The red soldiers produced by Nellie and Lilian in the house on Westbury Avenue with the Reg Aldridge die is the first remembered (unrecorded) item by Stephen Lowe. Only Stephen will recognise them (perhaps).

Book keeping started on 27/09/1946. This ledger was one of several Kemlows ledgers rescued from a skip by Stephen Lowe in 2001 just after the company was sold. There are no Kemlows records available after 01/05/1952.

Under the influence of Ray Jackson they bought an M55 machine (£130), die blocks (£26) and dies (£100) in 1946.

The first item produced by Kemlows was the Quad and this was invoiced on 27/09/1946 to Lullaby Toys, Muswell Hill. The Quad was a copy of an Austin 7. In real life the Austin was fixed with armour for the war effort.

Markings
Very few Kemlows products were marked as being made by them. It later became a marketing error by Charlie Kempster not to mark Kemlows products with a recognisable mark. Some early items were marked with one of the marks below.

Later Kemlows items were marked with "MADE IN ENGLAND" or "Made in England", sometimes in a rectangular box.

Bertie Ward (the MasterModels distributor - see later) in these later models was successful in eradicating any reference to Kemlows. Bertie Ward even went to the trouble of having "KEMLOWS" cold chiselled off the die used for the windmill.

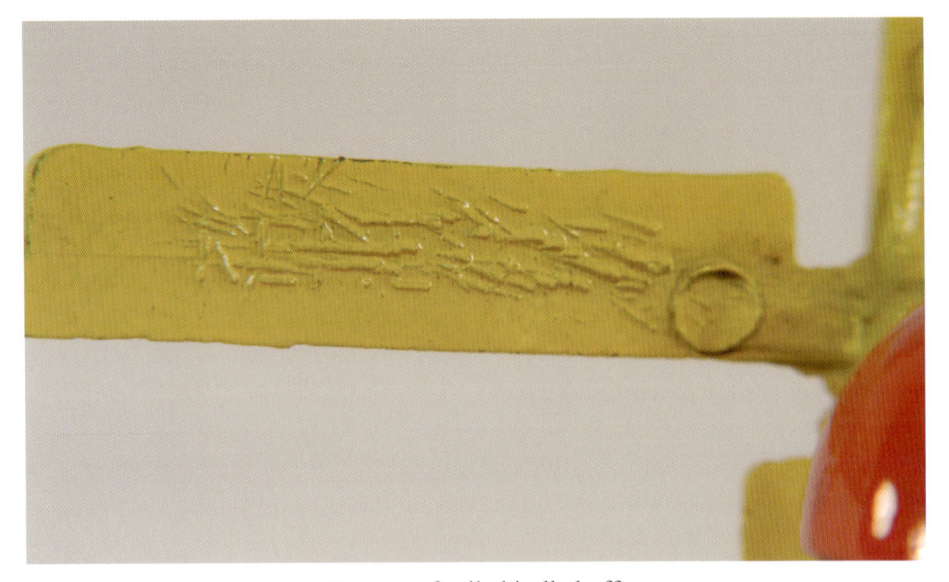

Reverse of sail chiselled off

Reverse of sail intact

EARLY PRODUCTS

If you are lucky you may find "KEMLOWS" intact on a very early (pre Wardie period) windmill.

The following are the early products of Kemlows from the initial ledger entry until the last recorded ledger entry on 01/05/1952. Prices given are the initial prices to wholesalers and shops. Prices did vary slightly depending on the amount supplied. Some prices will be missing as buyers bought in bulk and individual items are not costed - only the total. The amount sold is over the given period from the first to last entry for that item as recorded in the rescued ledgers.

Quad (Armoured Car) 27th September 1946 – 5th October 1946
1:60 scale. 12/- per dozen. 372 sold.

Unpainted base metal. Intended for children to paint their own camouflage. Some were painted olive green.

14 THE KEMLOW STORY

Quad and Gun 5th October 1946 – 25th October 1948
1:60 scale. 15/- per dozen. 50,589 sold.

As above, but with gun. For some orders the quad and gun were boxed singly for resale rather than in dozens. Vast sales.

Guns 17th June 1948 – 2nd July 1948
1:60 scale. 3/- per dozen. 71 sold.

The gun was sold on its own - but a small quantity at the end of the sales period.

Fleetmaster Saloon 3rd June 1947 – 25th June 1947
1:43 scale. 9/6 per dozen (later 9/-). 456 sold.

A new die was possibly introduced in March 1948 as ledgers then state "New Fleetmaster Saloon".

Base stamp

An actual Fleetmaster Saloon

Car and Caravan 2nd October 1947 – 11th January 1949
1:43 scale. 20/- per dozen. 31,567 sold.

The caravan has metal curtains as part of the design. Pearsons made the die for this.

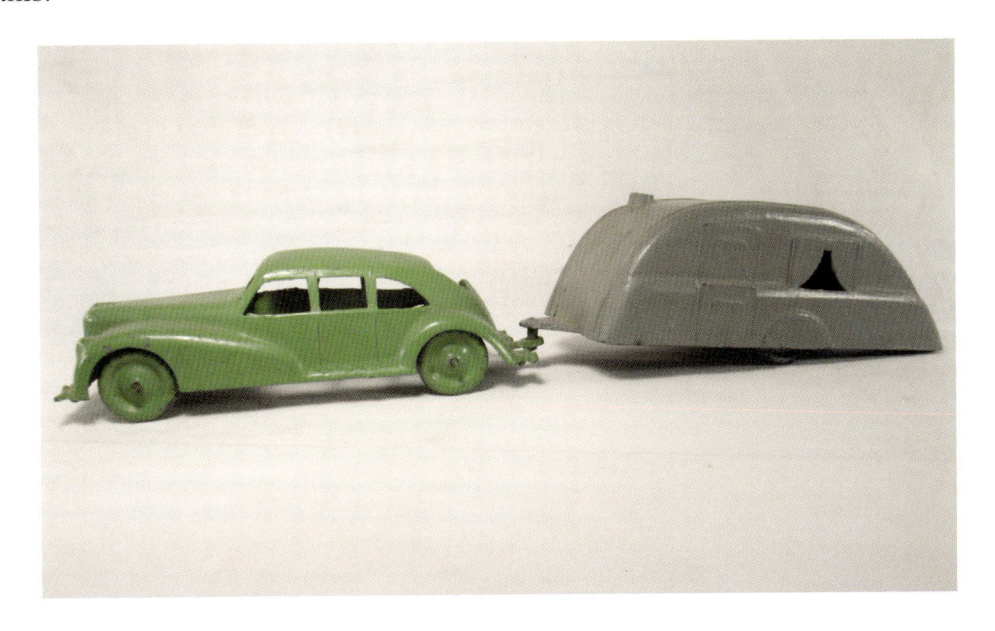

New Fleetmaster Saloon March 1948 – 22nd October 1948
1:43 scale. 9/- per dozen. 2,460 sold.

Caravan 17th June 1948 – 7th July 1948
1:43 scale. 10/- per dozen. 185 sold.

Cap Bombs 12th February 1948 – 1st January 1952
18/- per dozen (later 13/- per gross). 305,539 sold.

The two hemispheres are held together by a string wrapped around the groove. This traps a cap between the hemispheres. The bomb is then slung onto a hard surface. Quite an unnerving object.

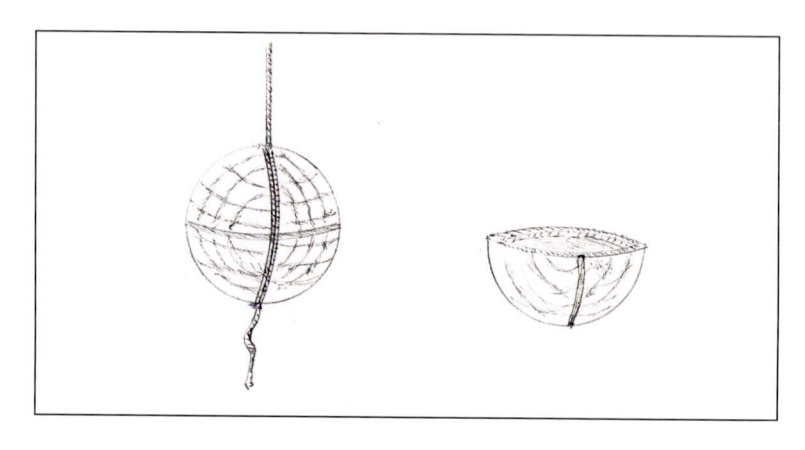

EARLY PRODUCTS

This is perhaps the total amount of sales as no more were sold in the last 5 months of the ledgers.

Randall (Merit) and Ward bought a lot of these at the end of this period. Perhaps these became an inspiration for the later plastic versions.

It is interesting to note that a Mr Oppenheimer bought 75,113 cap bombs – he just doesn't give up!!

Taxi 11th March 1948 – 25th October 1948
1:43 scale. 2, 874 sold.

This is thought to be a Fleetmaster with perhaps a taxi sign attached.
See variation on 11th September 1948.

Police Car 11th March 1948 – 4th February 1949
1:43 scale. 8/6 per dozen. 2,921 sold.

This is thought to be the Fleetmaster again with a police horn attached to the roof as on similar models of that period. Painted black.

Builder's Unit (Car and Trailer) 11th March 1948 – 11th January 1949
1:43 scale. 18/- per dozen. 5,746 sold.

This is a Fleetmaster saloon with a builder's trailer and ladder. The paper sign on the side of the trailer says "KEMLOWS BUILDERS".
"KEMLOWS. MADE IN ENGLAND" is cast into the underside of the trailer.
The trailer was later sold separately.

Note in this example, the ladder is missing

Clocks 2nd June 1948 – 23rd June 1948.
16/- per dozen. 42 only sold.

Nothing is known about this item. Very few were sold but 18 did go to a toy shop.

Builder's Trailer 17th June 1948 – 29th November 1948
1:43 scale. 9/- per dozen. 1,679 sold.

This was sold separately as there was a demand for this to go with the Fleetmaster saloon.

Yellow Cab 11th September 1948
1:43 scale. 7/- per dozen. 216 sold as one order.

This is a one-off order to Clive Products and is again perhaps a modified Fleetmaster.

Fences 25th October 1948 – 25th January 1951
Unknown scale. 18/- per gross. 28,272 sold.

BJ Ward bought 2,232 of these. Unidentified.

Gates 25th October 1948 – 23rd December 1950
Unknown scale. 15/- per gross. 16,572 sold.

BJ Ward bought 1,512 of these. Unidentified.

Stile 5th November 1948 – 6th December 1950
Unknown scale. 22/- per gross. 28,368 sold.

BJ Ward bought 2,604 of these. Unidentified.

Orchard Ladders 5th November 1948 – 6th December 1950
Unknown scale. 12/- per gross. 11,310 sold.

BJ Ward bought 228 only. Unidentified.

Bridges 12th November 1948 – 25th January 1951
Unknown scale. 30/- per gross. 32,760 sold.

BJ Ward bought 2,496 of these. The price suggests that this was not a substantial piece. Unidentified, but could possibly be the Monet style lead bridge mentioned earlier.

EARLY PRODUCTS

Swing Gates 19th November 1948 – 6th December 1950
Unknown scale. 21/- per gross (later 29/-). 31,836 sold.

BJ Ward bought 2,088 of these. Not the same as "Gates" as the prices are substantially different.

Signboard 7th January 1949 – 20th January 1951
Unknown scale. 13/- per gross. 13,410 sold.

BJ Ward bought 1,098 of these. The cost suggests these may be the signboards as in the MasterModels Track Signs or nameboard in the Track Accessories Set No 1.

Children on Seat 7th January 1949 – 5th December 1950
Unknown scale. 30/- per gross. 16,254 sold.

BJ Ward bought 2,136 of these. These were noted as "figures on seat", "children on seat" and "children" in the ledgers, but all ran for the same period and price. Currently unidentified.

Windmill 1st April 1949 – 10th December 1950
Scale: 3 $^5/_8''$ to top of vertical sail. 8/- per dozen. 13,116 sold.

BJ Ward bought 1,152. "KEMLOWS" on back of sail blade is usually found chiselled off as required by BJ Ward.

Name still intact

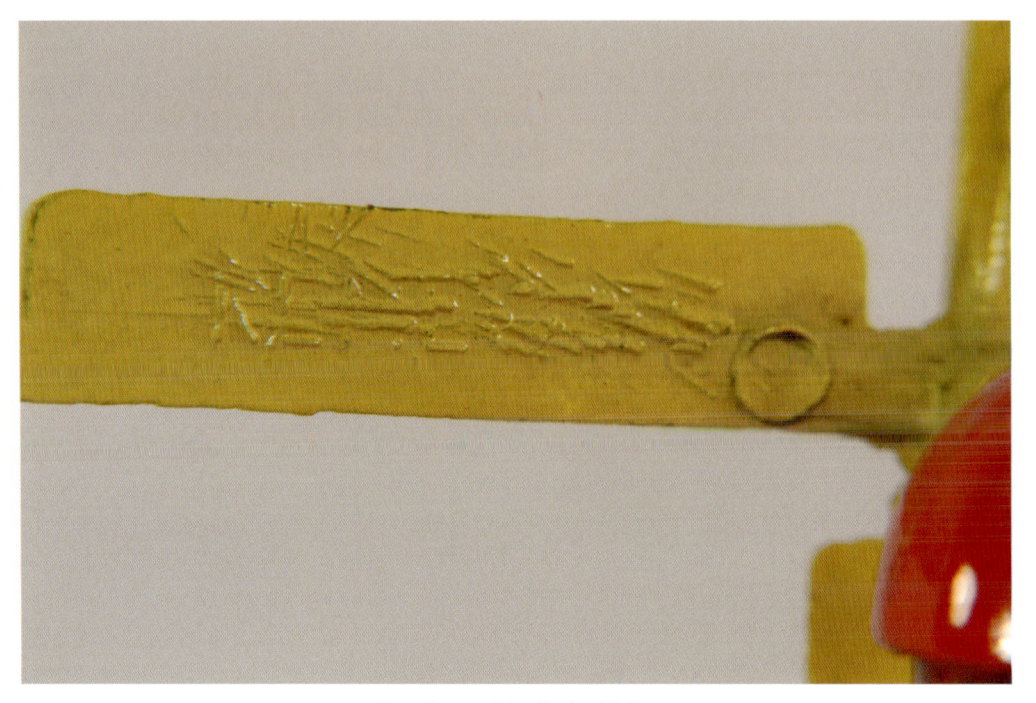

Kemlows chiselled off die

Rabbit Hutch 1st July 1949 – 8th November 1950
Unknown scale. 7/6 per dozen. 25,095 sold.

BJ Ward bought 1,440. Stephen Lowe suggests that casters and workers may have used their own naming of items rather than official names used by BJ Ward.

Seat 1st September 1949 – 7th September 1949
Unknown scale. 24/10 per gross. 1,152 sold.

The price and quantity indicate that these were remnants of "Children on Seat" sales. Only 8 gross sold.

Hurdle 9th December 1948 – 6th December 1950
Unknown item. 1,884 sold.

BJ Ward bought 348. This is not a stile as both appear on the same orders. A later order states "changing hurdles to gates" so suggests it is part of a gate.

Doll Casting 1st June 1950
30,000 sold to Sinclair on this date.

These are possibly the Pelham Poodle feet. Believed to be feet for Pelham Puppets, Wiltshire.

Dodgem (Sparking) Car 1st August 1950 – 10th December 1950
9/6 per dozen. 15,363 sold.

Thought in the past to be Crescent, but have been found in Kemlows ledgers. Stephen remembers the number transfers in sheets at home which were played with. Note that these were only sold over a two and a half month period, so if there were no further castings these would be rare. BJ Ward only bought 36, but FW Woolworth bought 1,512. The 'mast' screws vertically down into the back of the car and traps a flint in the vertical cavity against a knurled wheel on the car's rear wheel axle. On pushing the car, the flint 'sparks'.
Blue and red cars have been seen.

The following numbered sets appear in the MasterModels range. For full description see the MasterModels chapter.

The boy is not Kemlows, but perhaps Crescent

No 1 Track Accessories 10th December 1950 – 31st May 1951
Gauge 00. 17/- per dozen. 9,576 sold.

BJ Ward bought 3,024.
J Norman bought 5,544.
These were later sold through BJ Ward as MasterModels but they appeared, in various combinations advertised in the model railway press by other distributors.

No 1 Station Staff 10th December 1950 – 31st May 1951
Gauge 00. £5 per gross. 8/4 per dozen. 30,672 sold.

MasterModels Railway Staff Set 1. BJ Ward bought 24,480. This is the first time that BJ Ward is buying more of one item that anyone else.

Potato Gun 15th December1950 – 2nd April 1951
16/6 per gross. 114,984 sold.

All of these were bought by Sto Rose except for 8,640 (BJ Ward).

Entries from this point on have the second date bracketed. This is because production could have continued after this date, but of course there are no ledgers to support this.

No 2 Railway Passengers 22nd March 1951 – (1st April 1952)
Gauge 00. 11,748 sold to this date.

All sold to BJ Ward (exclusive sales for the first time).

No 3 Assorted Figures 15th March 1951 – (1st April 1952)
Gauge 00. 10,380 to this date, all to BJ Ward as "Set 3".

Note: Randall and Wood (Merit) bought 76,920 assorted figures. What happened to these very large orders? Could they have been absorbed in the British market, or even exported to the United States and sold as Aristo Tracksiders?

No 4 Seated Figures 15th May 1951 – (1st Feb 1952)
Gauge 00. 8,352 sold to this date, all to BJ Ward.

No 5 Seated Passengers 15th May 1951 – (1st April 1952)
Gauge 00. 7,430 sold to this date, all to BJ Ward.

No 6 Double Station Seat 2nd April 1951 – (1st April 1952)
Gauge 00. 7/10 per dozen. 5,916 sold to this date, all to BJ Ward.

No 7 Platform Accessories 15th May 1951 – (1st April 1952)
Gauge 00. 14,124 sold to this date, all to BJ Ward.

No 8 Milk Churns 1st June 1951 – (1st October 1951)
Gauge 00. 7,200 sold to this date, all to BJ Ward.

No 9 Level Crossing Gates 1st June 1951 – (1st April 1952)
Gauge 00. 9,444 sold to this date, all to BJ Ward.

No 10 Platform Equipment Set 27th August 1951 – (1st April 1952)
Gauge 00. 12/6 per dozen. 5,856 sold to this date, all to BJ Ward.

No 10 Platform Equipment Set (Improved) 27th August 1951 – (1st April 1952)
Gauge 00. 2,352 sold to this date, all to BJ Ward.

Contents of Set 10 did vary, but there was no indication which one was the "improved" set.

Large Puppet Hands 1st October 1951 – 1st May 1952
£15 13s per thousand. 21,770 sold to Pelham Puppets, Wiltshire.

Small Puppet Hands 1st October 1951 – 1st May 1952
£12 5s 6d per thousand. 29,900 sold to Pelham Puppets, Wiltshire.

No 11 Gradient Posts 1st November 1951 – (1st April 1952)
Gauge 00. 300 sold to this date, all to BJ Ward.

No 12 Electric Trolley Set 2nd November 1951 – (1st April 1952)
Gauge 00. 8/- per dozen. 7,344 sold to this date, all to BJ Ward.

No 14 WH Smith Kiosk 2nd November 1951 – (1st April 1952)
Gauge 00. 1,704 sold to this date, all to BJ Ward.

No 15 Telephone Booths 10th December 1951 – (1st April 1952)
Gauge 00. 2,964 sold to this date, all to BJ Ward.

No 16 Station Lamps 1st March 1952 – (1st April 1952)
Gauge 00. 463 sold to this date, all to BJ Ward.

No 17 Girders 1st October 1951 – (4th December 1951)
Gauge 00. 2,426 sold to this date, all to BJ Ward.

EARLY PRODUCTS

Only sold over a 3 month period, but could have been sold after April 1952. As these were only advertised once though, these are perhaps the total sales.

No 18 Cable Drums 10th December 1951 – (1st April 1952)
Gauge 00. 8/6 per dozen. 4,763 sold to this date, all to BJ Ward.

No 19 Tar Barrels 10th December 1951 – (1st April 1952)
Gauge 00. 4/4 per dozen. 7,590 sold to this date, all to BJ Ward.

No 20 Oil Barrels 10th December 1951 – (1st April 1952)
Gauge 00. 3,081 sold to this date, all to BJ Ward.

Pumps 1st January 1951 – (1st May 1952)
28,596 sold to this date, all to BJ Ward.

Sold in set no 44.

No 21 Platform Gardens 1st March 1952 – (1st April 1952)
Gauge 00. 2,892 sold to this date, all to BJ Ward.

No 22 Platform Gardens 1st March 1951 – (1st April 1952)
Gauge 00. 2,388 sold to this date, all to BJ Ward.

No 23 Track Party 1st April 1952 – (1st May 1952)
Gauge 00. 1,404 sold in these two months, all to BJ Ward.

No 24 Police Boxed 1st February 1952 – (1st April 1952)
Gauge 00. 2,892 sold in these three months, all to BJ Ward.

Bus Stops 1st March 1952 – (1st April 1952)
1,428 sold in these two months, all to BJ Ward.

No 25 Placards 1st April 1952 – (1st May 1952)
Gauge 00. 1,512 sold in these two months, all to BJ Ward.

No 26 Sleeper Buffer 1st April 1952 – (1st May 1952)
Gauge 00. 1,452 sold in these two months, all to BJ Ward.

Oil Cabinets 1st April 1952 – (1st May 1952)
Gauge 0. 1,884 sold in these two months, all to BJ Ward.

K13 individually boxed and K66 box of 1 dozen, from the K series (see later).

ESSO sign 1st April 1952 – (1st May 1952)
Gauge 0. 5/7 per dozen. 1,020 sold in these two months, all to BJ Ward.

These are K12 from the K Series (see later).

No 31 Enquiry Kiosks 1st May 1952 (only)
Gauge 00. 360 sold on this date, all to BJ Ward.

After this date, no Kemlows records exist, so production is tracked though the toy literature / adverts / sales promotions of the period.

See Appendix for the items made by Kemlows during this early period that are non-toy related.

Three

The B J Ward Influence

Looking at the production of Kemlows toys in the last chapter, it becomes clear that BJ Ward got to the stage in 1952 when he was buying vast amounts of Kemlows items.

B J Ward Ltd (Bertie John) started business in 1946 as a wholesaler. It appears that he took any opportunity of supplying the toy market with anything he could. This trend continued in to the 1960s. His major success though was with Kemlows, and with what became known in 1951 as the MasterModels range.

Marketing was his strong point. Today many people think that MasterModels were made by B J Ward Ltd - nothing further from the truth. Kemlows were completely eradicated from the sales literature that Bertie Ward had produced. Their name was even chiselled off the dies for the early windmills.

Some of the items in addition to MasterModels should be noted though as Bertie Ward did bring them to prominence.

In the MasterModels Catalogue and Handbooks produced in 1955, 1956 and 1958, other items sold were the Kemlows Garage Equipment Series (The "K Series" - see the later chapter on the K series).

One of the most popular and collectable series advertised in the Handbooks are the Woodside, Rickwood and Clarewood model railway buildings.

I am still researching the company who made these. Suffice to say that the myth about Rickwood and Clarewood being named after the manufacturer's children is untrue. So is any connection with the RAF.

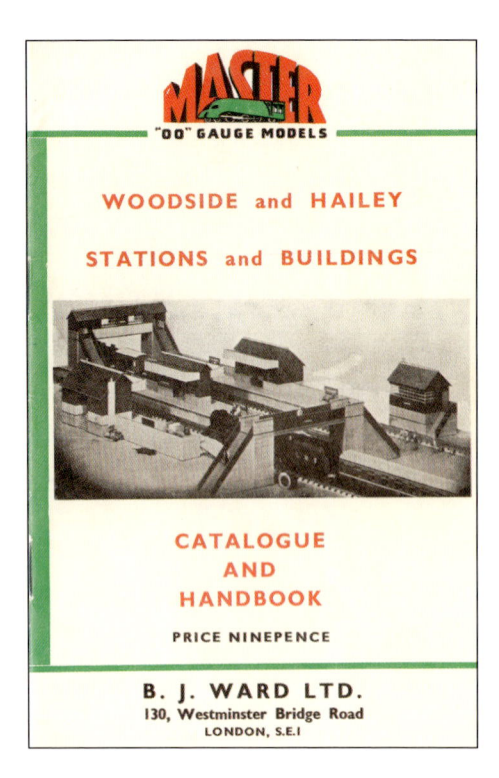

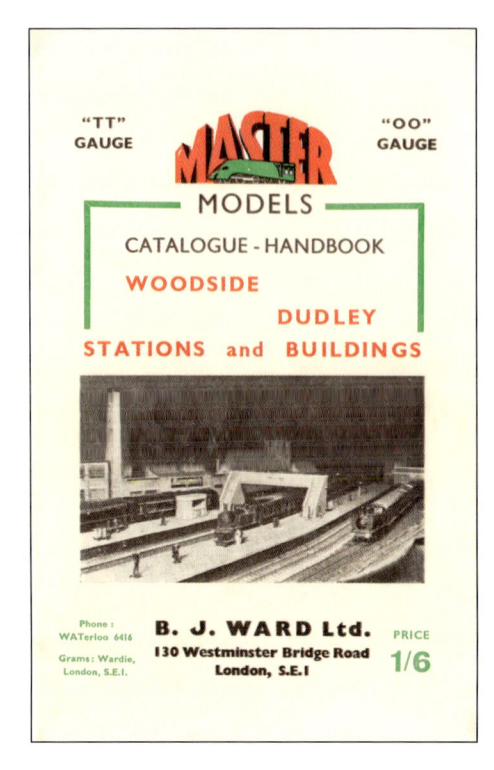

Sept 1955

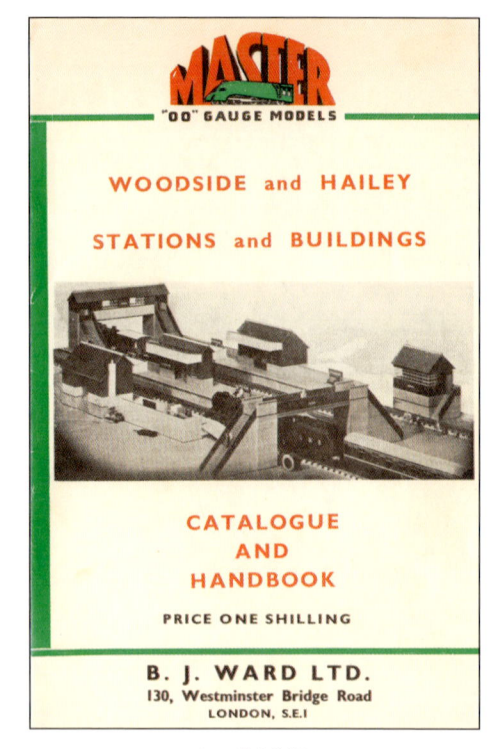

April 1956

February 1958

The Hailey Series of wooden model railway buildings was heavily advertised by Bertie Ward in these Handbooks and in other literature.

The company was a prolific manufacturer starting production in 1922 at Queens Road, Brighton, moving to the Southern Region Goods Depot on Sackville Road, Hove in 1932. A full history of the company is in print[1].

Dudley Toys of Dudley Road, Eastbourne produced a limited range of wooden model railway buildings advertised in the 1958 Handbook. No history can be found of this company except that Dudley Road in the 1950s had many garages used by craftsmen, producing such items.

Bertie also advertised his Wardie Series of tunnels, road bridges etc. made of card and flock. Many were stamped "WARDIE" or "A WARDIE PRODUCT" in black ink.

Tudor and modern style buildings made of wood were also advertised, so were Puck Scenery (made of sponge rubber) made by Grovewell Ltd.

A big seller was Gilco Traffic Signs, which were well illustrated in the Handbooks. These were made in Birmingham by Giltoy Products Limited, owned by Gilbert Whitehouse, and were delivered by Gilbert regularly to BJ Ward's warehouse in London. A history of the company's production of road signs is in print[2].

BJ Ward was based at 130 Westminster Bridge Road for the majority of the time, a small shop frontage with a very high kerb outside. Barry Whitehouse, son of the owner of Giltoy Products Ltd, remembers as a small boy helping his dad deliver Gilco signs, always tripping up this very high kerb. He points out that Gilco box lids always seemed to be split half way down the lid on both sides. This was due to his dad holding bundles of boxes together with string and Barry dropping them!

BJ Ward's address in the late 1940s was Westminster Warehouses, but at 130 Westminster Bridge Road. I do have an address at 224 Grand Buildings, Trafalgar Square in January 1950, until at least February 1951.

Interestingly, the MasterModel Water Tower (WT) advertised in 1951 had an address of Thornton Heath, Surrey printed on the box. I've not solved this one as of yet, but in the 1950s Thornton Heath was a quaint idyllic residential area with its village pond etc. Perhaps Bertie had either family or outwork connections there that encouraged him to use this prestigious address.

In addition to his handbooks, BJ Ward advertised MasterModels widely through his own flyers and distributed these to toy companies and shops with their own names and addresses on, e.g. Southgate Hobbies, Hamleys, A.N. Hales, Bradshaw Model Products etc.

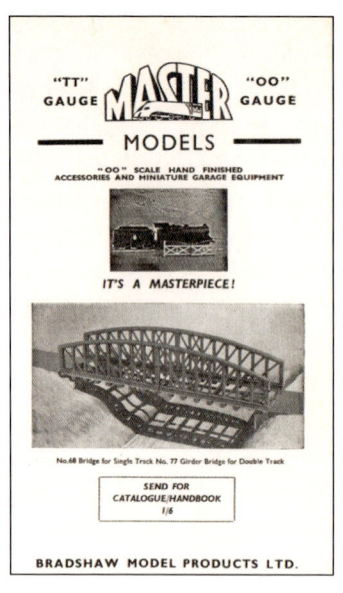

Three leaf fold

Early flyer

Later flyer

Toy companies in their own right advertised MasterModels throughout the 1950s. Notably Gamages, Bradshaw Model Products (BMP), The Model Railway Handbook and Hobbies Handbook. Many smaller shops advertised every month in the model railway press (mainly the Model Railway News) as being a source for MasterModels.

BJ Ward used the Model Railway News many times in the 1950s to advertise MasterModels.

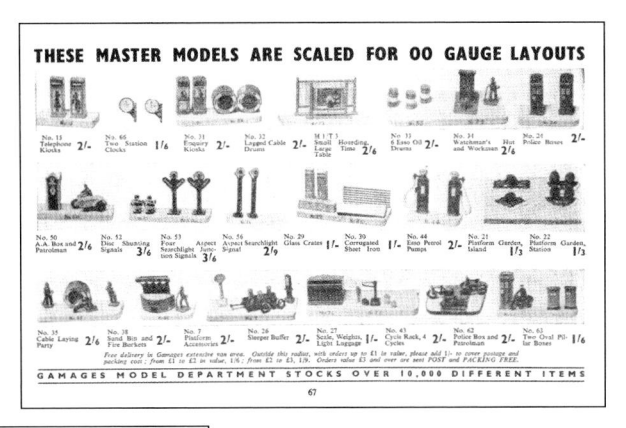

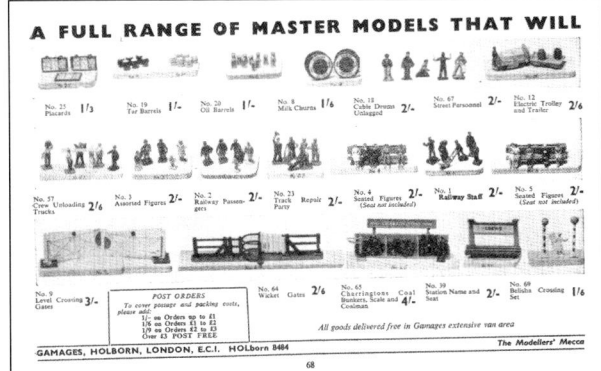

Gamages Catalogue 1955

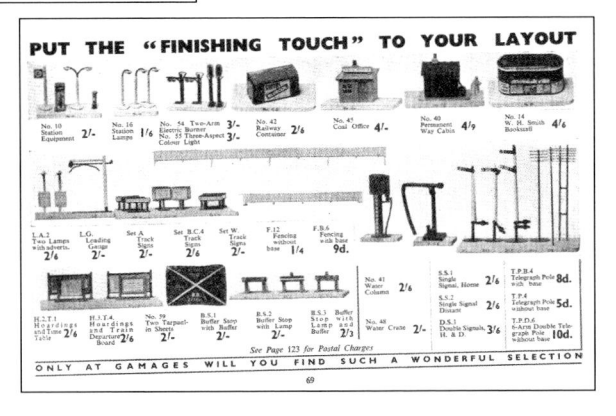

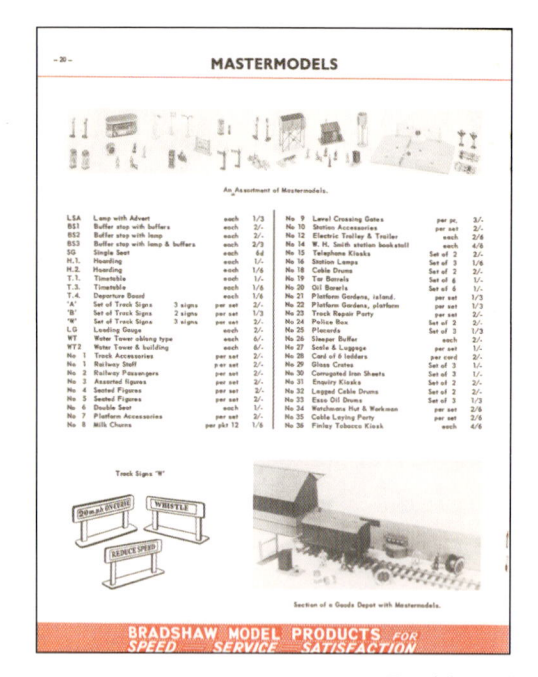

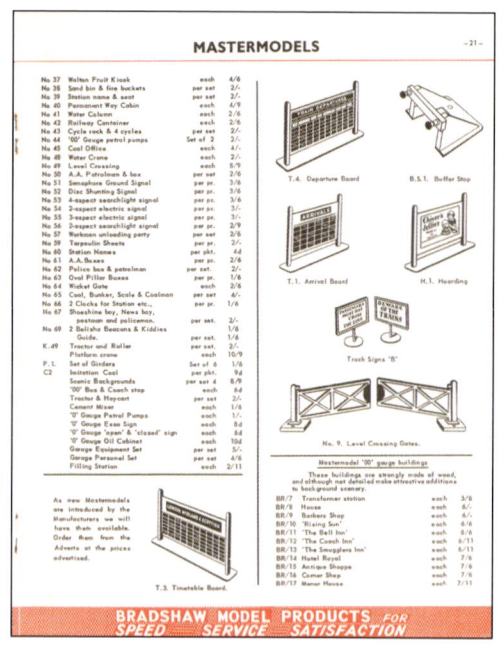

Bradshaw Catalogue 1954/5

Four

The MasterModel Range

The whole range was advertised and distributed by BJ Ward.

Manufacturers supplied Bertie Ward with the goods and he did the rest.

The closest I have got to an image of Bertie Ward is from Peter and Joy Cowan who now live in the United States. In the 1950s, Peter and Joy emigrated to Canada, but Joy returned on a business trip to see Bertie Ward to become the sole distributors of MasterModels in Canada.

She describes him as a double for Rumpole of the Bailey!
Kemlows diecasting provided the majority of the MasterModel range, but Bertie Ward did put non-Kemlows items in the range (e.g. the wooden block buildings).

For completion's sake, all items will be included to give a complete listing of MasterModels.

As seen in the last chapter, the Kemlows / Ward relationship developed in the early 1950s, but Ward was dealing with other suppliers, just before the Kemlows relationship developed, notably Don Bowles of Croydon.

Don Bowles was an engineer dealing in model railways and made his own railway accessories from brass. His first advert appeared in The Model Railway News in July 1950 advertising "REALISTIC MODELS" in '00'.

This was soon followed by an advert in the Games and Toys Year Book for 1951, from BJ Ward. Note all the loose items are Don Bowles items.

Don Bowles items July 1950

Games and Toys ad 1951

BJ Ward followed this by another advert in the Model Railway News in February 1951.

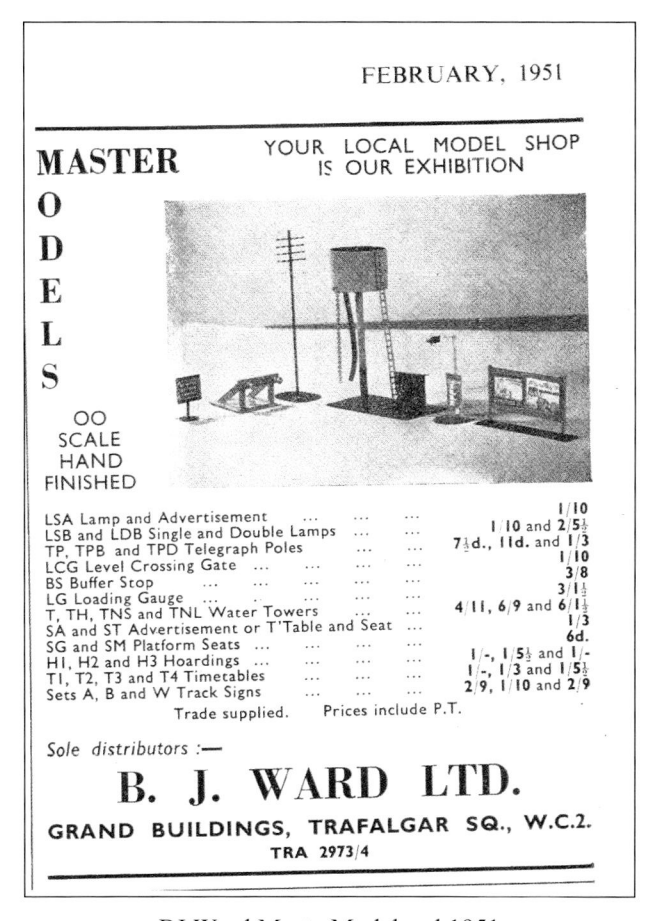

```
                                    FEBRUARY, 1951

MASTER        YOUR LOCAL MODEL SHOP
              IS OUR EXHIBITION
O
D
E
L
S

  OO
  SCALE
  HAND
  FINISHED
                                                              1/10
  LSA Lamp and Advertisement         ...    ...    ...   1/10 and 2/5½
  LSB and LDB Single and Double Lamps ...   ...   7½d., 11d. and 1/3
  TP, TPB and TPD Telegraph Poles    ...    ...    ...        1/10
  LCG Level Crossing Gate   ...      ...    ...    ...         3/8
  BS Buffer Stop   ...      ...      ...    ...    ...         3/1½
  LG Loading Gauge  ...     ...      ...    ...    ...   4/11, 6/9 and 6/1½
  T, TH, TNS and TNL Water Towers    ...    ...                1/3
  SA and ST Advertisement or T'Table and Seat  ...              6d.
  SG and SM Platform Seats  ...      ...    ...    1/-, 1/5½ and 1/-
  H1, H2 and H3 Hoardings   ...      ...    ...    1/-, 1/3 and 1/5½
  T1, T2, T3 and T4 Timetables       ...    ...    2/9, 1/10 and 2/9
  Sets A, B and W Track Signs        ...    ...
              Trade supplied.    Prices include P.T.

Sole distributors :—
          B. J. WARD LTD.
    GRAND BUILDINGS, TRAFALGAR SQ., W.C.2.
                  TRA 2973/4
```

BJ Ward MasterModels ad 1951

Note again these are all Don Bowles items. It was not long before Don Bowles was overtaken by BJ Ward. Indeed it is easy to see later the similarities between some of the Don Bowles hand made items and the Kemlows (BJ Ward) cast items. Many of the early MasterModels advertised by BJ Ward were indeed Don Bowles hand made items.

The relationship between BJ Ward and Don Bowles was strained as Don Bowles felt his range was being marketed and developed independently of himself. Not long after, in 1951, Don Bowles gave up his hand made work and moved to Tiverton in Devon to become a model railway retailer.

The MasterModel range, K-series, Sentry Box Series and Master Series grew out of a combination of model railway engineers making products for a hungry post-war toy-starved market, a skilled diecasting company wanting to expand and a marketing entrepreneur.

The listing

In the MasterModels listings below you will find the following headings format: *Set letter or number. Set name. Number of items in set. Dates between which the item was advertised. Price range. Scarcity.*

Date: If the Kemlows sales ledger date is known, the date is followed by a K, e.g. 1951K means the item was sold by Kemlows in 1951.
Price range: These are the known retail prices on release and subsequently.

Intergranular Corrosion: You will more than likely find in the early casting examples of this type of corrosion. It exhibits itself by tiny cracks and splits in the cast object. This will then result in a twisting of the item. The early trackside items e.g. buffer stops, Set A, Set B, Set C and Set W suffered from this problem. The problem is caused by too much lead in the metal. A 0.1% impurity is enough to create the problem. The lead acts as a lubricant and the casting eventually slips. It sometimes takes 20 years to show itself. In the trade, this type of metal was called Monkey Metal.

MasterModel Lettered Sets Listing

Including Don Bowles designs and other BJ Ward (Wardie) items.

BBS/1   See other Wardie items at end

BBS/2   See other Wardie items at end

BC4 Track Signs   4. 1955,1960. 2/6. Quite scarce in box.

Track signs (grey or fawn). This is a composite set of Set B and Set C.

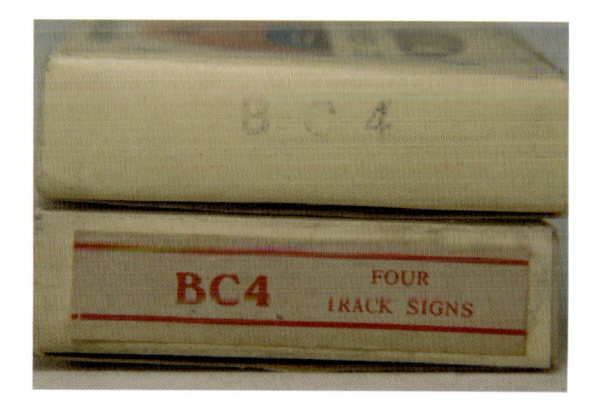

THE MASTER MODEL RANGE

BS Buffer Stop   1. 1951. 3/8. Scarce.
Buffer stop with buffers designed by Don Bowles and advertised by BJ Ward.

BS1 Buffer Stop   1. 1950. 3/8. Scarce.
Buffer stop with lamp but no buffers designed by Don Bowles and advertised by him.

BS1 Buffer Stop with Buffers   1. 1951,1957. 2/-. Quite common.
Cast buffer stop (grey), buffer bar (red) and buffer (grey).
Cast by Kemlows, not a Don Bowles hand made design.

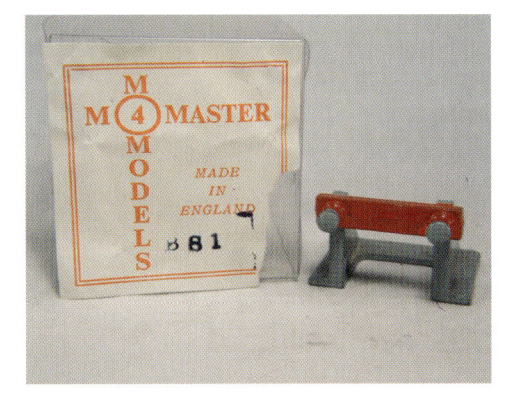

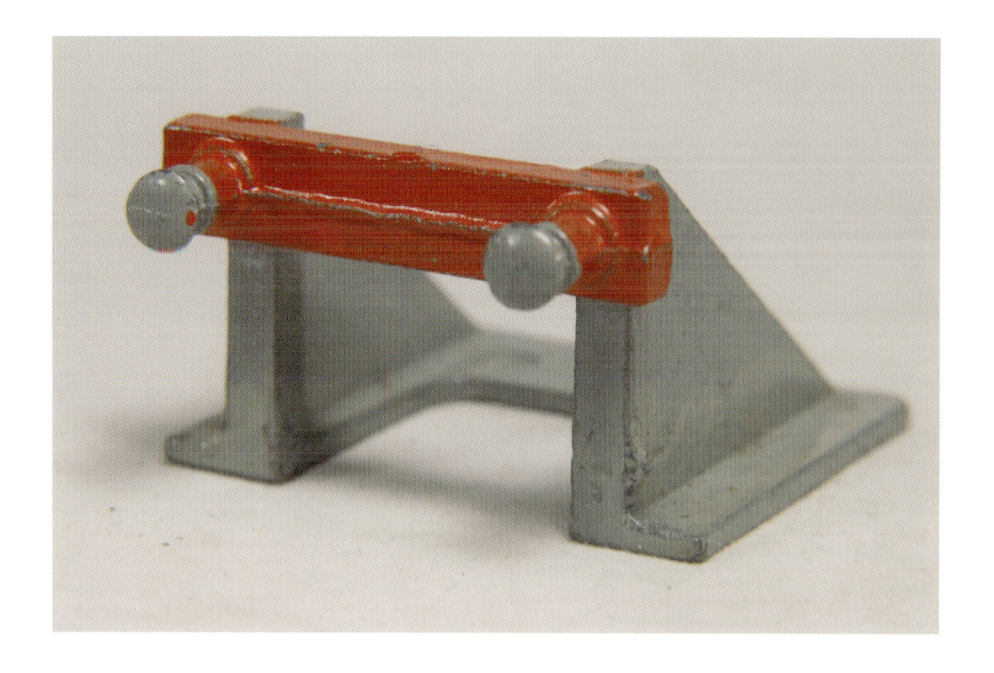

BS2 Buffer Stop with Lamp   1. 1951,1960. 2/-. Quite common.
Cast buffer stop (grey), buffer bar (red). No buffers, but a lamp (red).

BS3 Buffer Stop with Lamp and Buffer　　1.　1952.　2/3.　Quite common.
As BS1 and BS2 but with buffers and lamp.

C2 Imitation Coal Packet.　　1952,1960.　9d.　Very scarce.
Imitation coal in 'double' size packet from a shop display card of 12.

D3   See Posters

DP   See under Telegraph Poles

DS3 Double Signal (Home and Distant)   1. 1952,1953. 3/6. Very scarce. Was originally called DS in 1950. Designed by Don Bowles. In January 1954, was listed as discontinued.

ES Electric Signal   1. 1952. 12/6. Very scarce.

F1 Steel Girders   See set 17 in MasterModel listings.

F6   See FB6.

F12 Spring Wire Fencing without base (12")   6. 1951. 1/4. Very scarce.

FB6 Spring Wire Fencing with base (6")   6. 1952,1957. 9d each strip. Very scarce.

Half dozen wrapped in brown paper, but sold separately.
Was F6 in 1951.
These wire fencings could have been produced by Don Bowles as they were hand made.

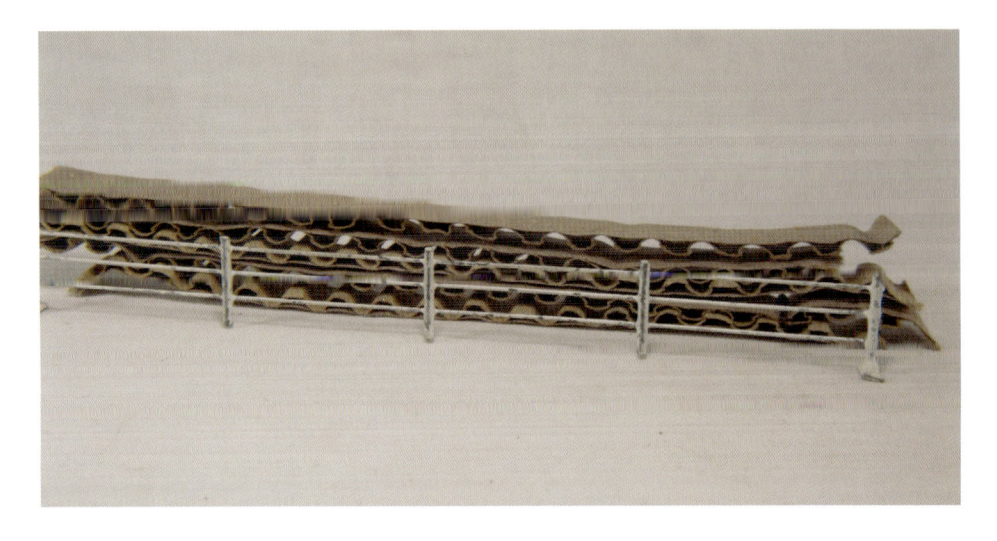

Hoardings

H1 Hoarding   1. 1951,1954. 1/-. Common.

Small hoarding (grey or green) with coloured advert.

THE KEMLOW STORY

H2 Hoarding 1. 1951, 1961. Quite common.

Large hoarding (grey, green, fawn or black) with two coloured adverts.

H3 Hoarding Warning Notice 1. 1951, 1953. Quite common.

Small hoarding (grey, green or red) with "BRITISH RAILWAYS", "WARNING", "TRESPASSERS WILL BE PROSECUTED", "BY ORDER". Is also part of H3 / T4 set.

H3 Hoarding Warning Notice   1. 1951. Very scarce.

Small black hoarding.

I suspect this is rare, as it is the only one I've seen in nearly 20 years. A Don Bowles design.

H1/T3 Small Hoarding and Large Timetable   2. 1955,1959. 2/6. Quite common.

Small hoarding (grey) with coloured advert. Large hoarding (grey or green) with timetable.

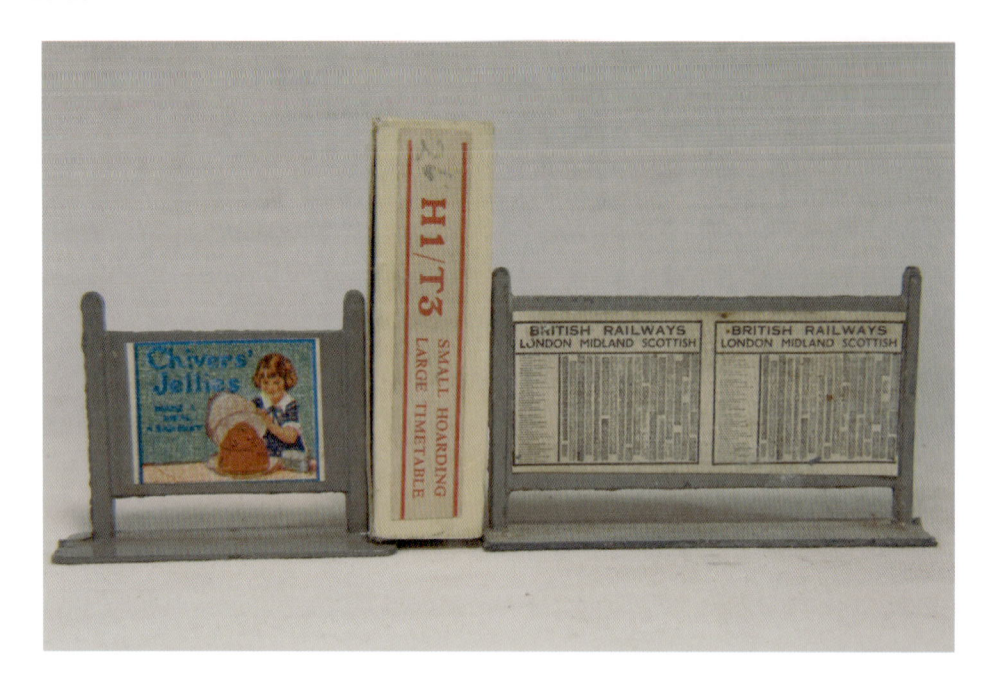

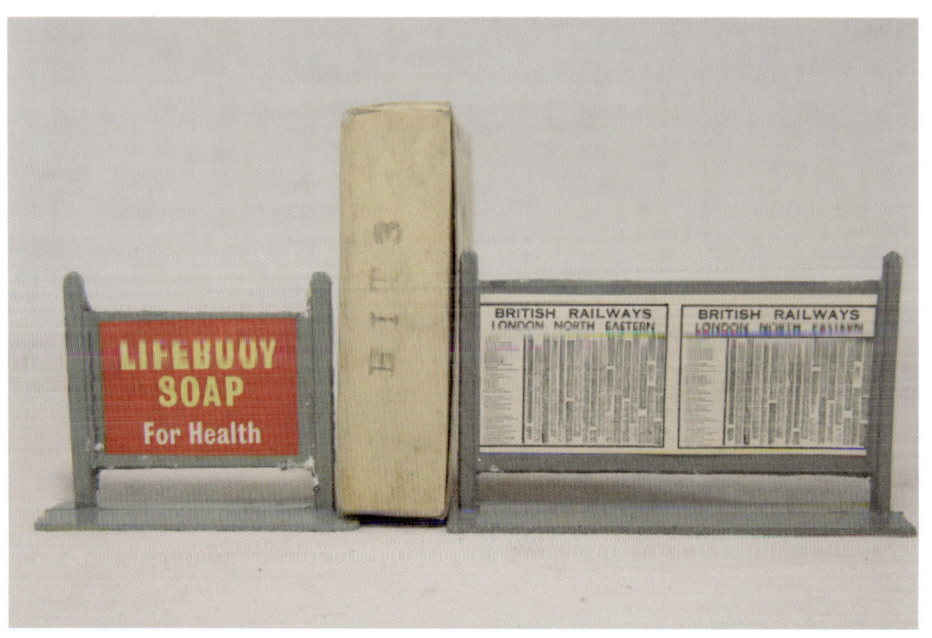

H2/T1 Large hoarding and Small Timetable   2.   1955,1961.   2/6.   Quite common.

Large hoarding (grey, green or fawn) with two coloured adverts. Small hoarding (grey or red oxide) with timetable.

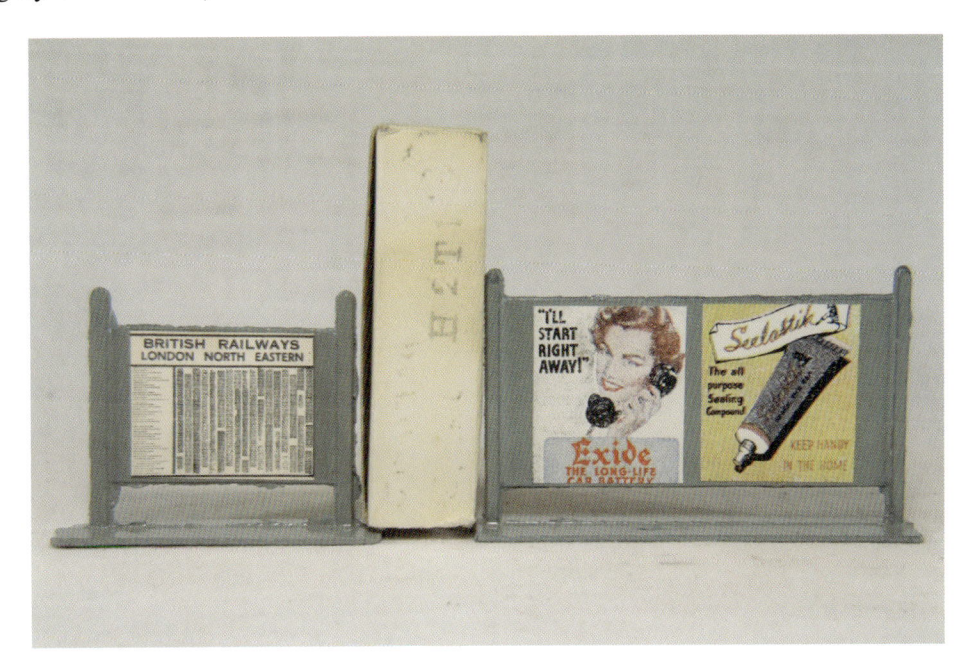

H3/T4 Warning Notice and Departure Board 2. 1955,1959. 2/6. Quite common.

Small hoarding (grey or green) with Warning notice from H3, with large departure board.

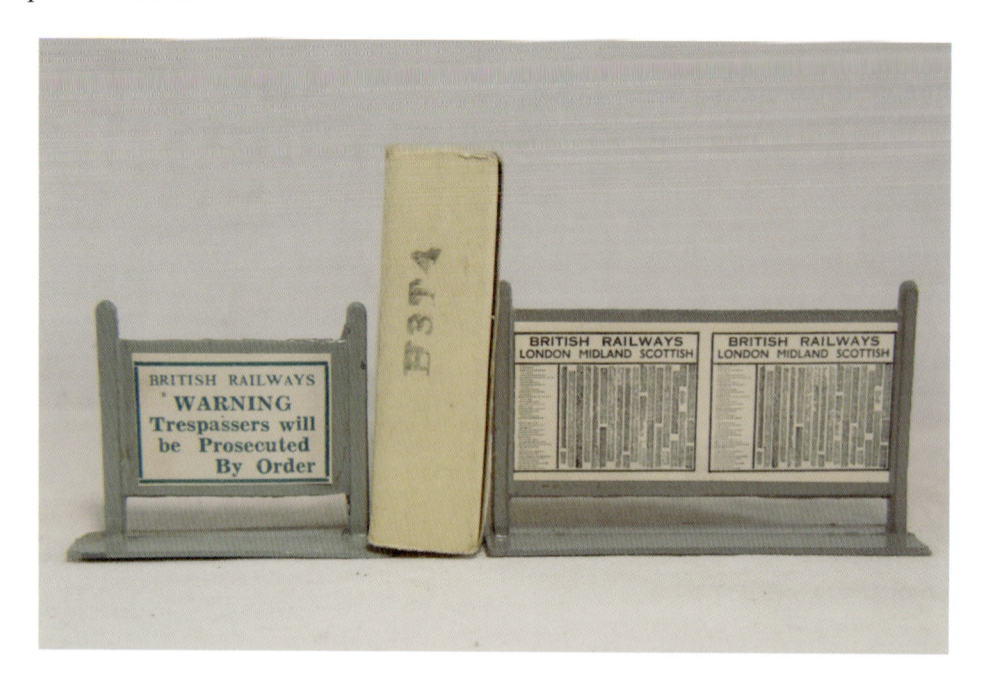

LA2 Lamp and Advert   2. 1955, 1961. 2/6. Quite scarce with box.
Two lamps of the same colour (grey or mushroom) with printed adverts.
Was LSA 1951-1955, which were in individual packets instead.

LCG Level Crossing Gates   2. 1951,1952. 1/10. Scarce.
These initial single track gates appeared in a BJ Ward advert selling Don Bowles items.
Cast items appear in 1952 as Set 9.

LDB Double Lamp   1. 1951. 2/5 ½. Very scarce in packet.
Deleted same year.

LG Loading Gauge   1. 1950,1951. 2/-. Quite scarce.
This was a Don Bowles design renumbered and redesigned (not as fine) to No 80 in 1953.

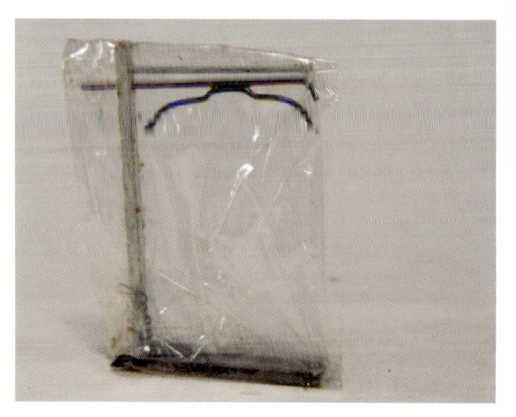

THE MASTER MODEL RANGE 51

LL1 Lighting Lamp   1950. 6/3. Scarce.

A Don Bowles hand made item. Advertised by Don Bowles.

LSA Lamp with Single Advert

1. 1951,1955. 1/3. Scarce in packet. Earlier release of LA2, but sold individually in a packet.

LSB Single Lamp

1. 1950,1951. Very scarce. A Don Bowles design with LNER timetable. Deleted 1951.

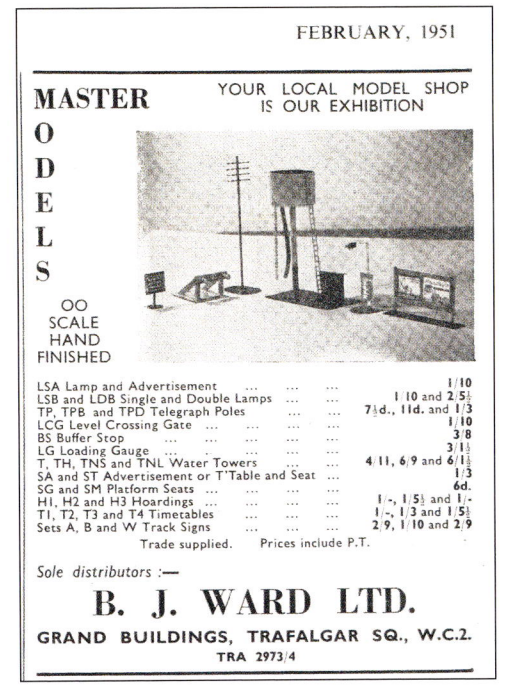

second from right

00 Gauge Bus and Coach Stop   4.1953,1959. Very scarce.

This early packaging has not been seen yet. Unlikely that Set 94 is the same casting.

PL1 New Universal Plus Point Lever   1. 1958. 2/-. Very scarce in packet.

Three-sixteenths of an inch throw.

Many companies made this item in the early 1950s. One in BJ Ward packaging is yet to be seen.

Q1 Imitation Quarry Granite   Packet. 1956,1961. 9d. Very scarce.

Imitation quarry packets from a shop display card of 12.

RC1 Rail Cleaner   1. 1960,1961. 6d. Very scarce in packet.

3" grey cleaner in packet. This would look like many other manufacturer's rail cleaners, but was packaged for BJ Ward.

This must be considerably rare in its original packet.

SA Advertisement   1. 1951. 1/3. Very scarce in packet.
Don Bowles small brass hoarding, painted black. Paper advert.

Set A Track Signs   3. 1951,1959. 2/-, 2/9. Quite common.
Small sign boards. All grey or all green.
These are often found suffering from metal fatigue due to faulty casting at the time.

Set A Track Signs   3. 1950. Rare.
A rare unusual set designed by Don Bowles. Hand made in brass.

Set B Track Signs   2. 1951,1961. 1/3, 1/10. Quite common.

Track signs in grey (see BC4) are often found suffering from metal fatigue due to faulty casting at the time.

Set C Track Signs   2. 1951,1957. 1/3, 2/9. Quite common.

Track signs in grey (see BC4) are often found suffering from metal fatigue due to faulty casting at the time.

Set W1 Track Signs   3. 1951. Scarce.

"REDUCE SPEED", "WHISTLE" and "20 MPH ON CURVE".

A Don Bowles design.

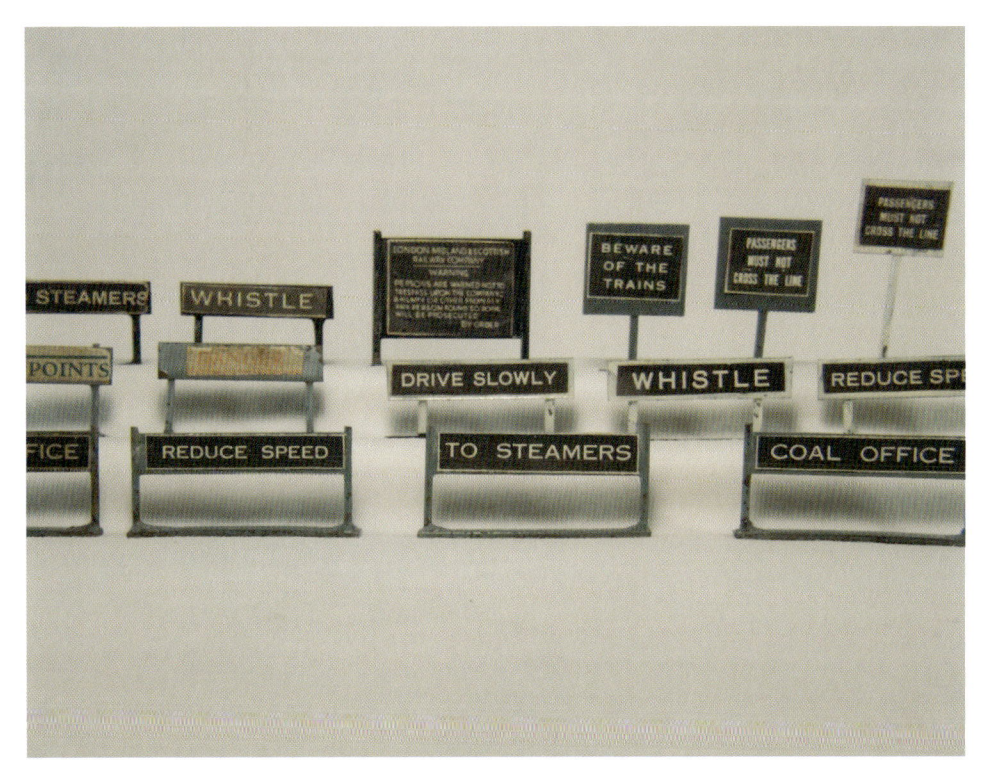

Two seen here

Set W Track Signs   3. 1951,1953. 2/-, 2/9. Quite common.

Track signs (3 grey, 3 green or 3 cream).

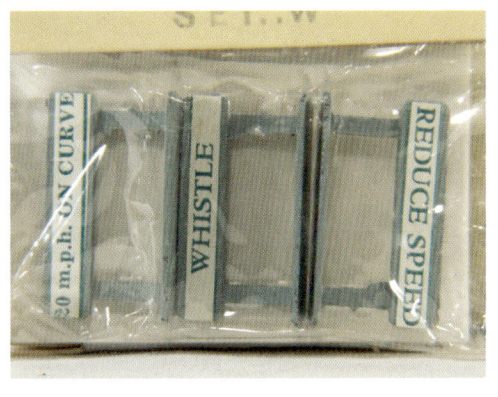

SG Single Seat 1. 1951,1953. 6d. Scarce.

One single grey platform seat. Same as in SG4.

SG4 Single Seats 4. 1955,1959. 2/-. Quite common.

Four single grey platform seats.

SM Single Seat   1. 1951,1953. 6d. Scarce.

One single green seat. Packets of three sold separately.

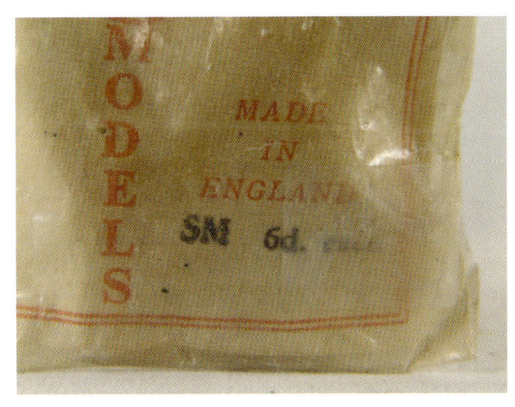

SM4 Single Seats   4. 1955,1959. 2/-. Quite common.

Four single green platform seats.

S1 Single Arm Signal (Home or distant)   1. 1950. 2/9. Rare.

A Don Bowles design, advertised by Don Bowles.

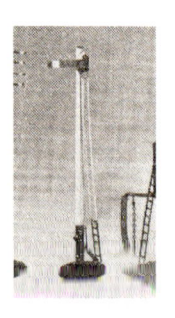

S2 Double Arm Signal (Home or distant)   1. 1950. 4/4. Rare.

A Don Bowles design, advertised by Don Bowles.

SS Single Signal (Home or distant)   1. 1952. 2/6. Rare.

A relettering by BJ Ward of Don Bowles' S1.

SS1 Single Signal (Home)   1. 1950, 1953. 2/6. Rare.

A Don Bowles design, relettered by BJ Ward (was S1, then SS).

SS2 Single Signal (Distant)   1. 1950, 1953. Rare.

A Don Bowles design, relettered by BJ Ward (was S1, then SS).

ST Timetable and Seat   1. 1951. 1/3. Very rare in packet.

A Don Bowles item made from brass sheet. This green variety is seen in a BJ Ward original packet. Grey has also been seen.

THE MASTER MODEL RANGE 59

Timetables

T1 Timetable   1. 1951,1955. 1/-. Quite common. Small hoarding with train timetable. Green, grey or maroon. 1 $^{3}/_{16}$″ by $^{13}/_{16}$″ board.

THE MASTER MODEL RANGE   61

T2 Timetable   1. 1951. 1/3. Scarce.

Timetable introduced and deleted in 1951.

1 ⅝" by 1" board. Slightly bigger than T1. Round wire posts.

A Don Bowles design.

T3 Timetable   1. 1951,1955. 1/5 ½,1/7. Quite common.

Large timetable.

T4 Departure Board   1. 1951,1955. 1/5 ½, 1/7. Quite common.
Large departure timetable.

Assorted Don Bowles Designs   1949,1951. All quite scarce.

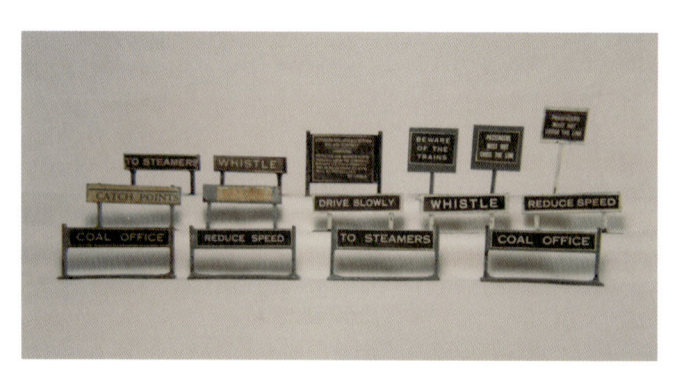

Telegraph Poles

These were first seen advertised by Don Bowles in July 1950 made from fabricated steel with four arms and labelled T.P.1. Over the next few years, various combinations of poles appeared. Two arm, four arm, six arm, single post, double post, with or without bases. These were identical in presentation and many must have been made as they are still available today. It could be the case that after 1954 and Don Bowles' withdrawal from manufacturing, another company (or several) took over production.

00 Telegraph Pole   1. 1954. Quite scarce.

Steel wire telegraph pole, black, with two (sometimes called Type A) or three arms.

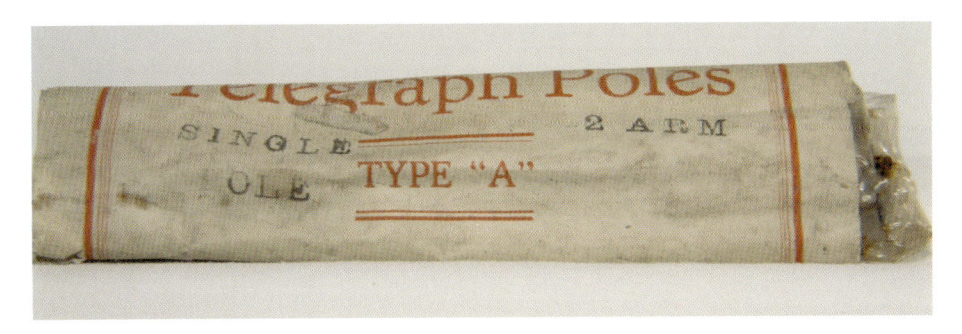

TP6 Telegraph Pole   1. 1950,1952. 10d. Quite scarce.

Steel wire double telegraph pole, black, with six arms. Poles joined by two cross pieces. No base. Later called TPD6 (1952). Listed also as TPD and DP6 Arm (six in this packet).

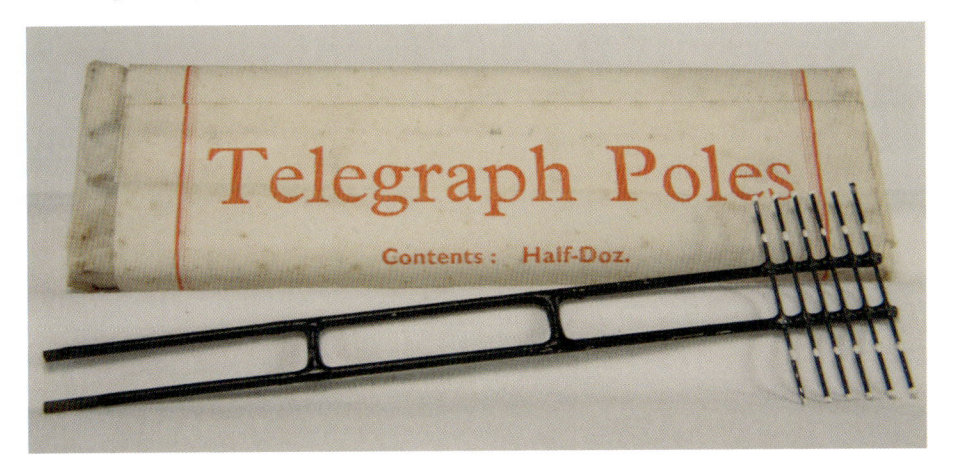

TP Telegraph Pole   1. 1950,1952. 5 ½d, 7 ½d . Quite scarce.
Steel wired telegraph pole, black, with four arms. Later called TP4 (1952).

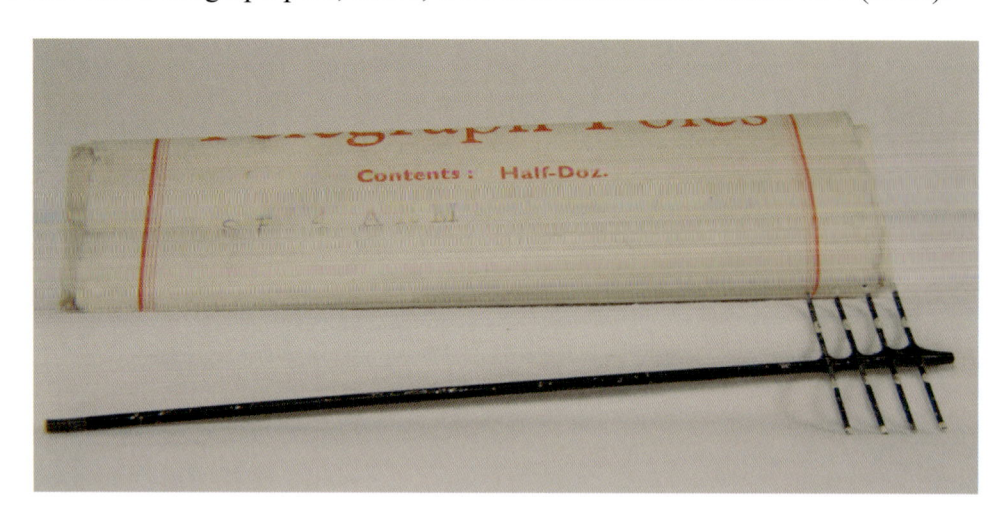

TPB Telegraph Pole   1. 1950,1952. 8 ½d, 11d. Quite scarce.
Steel wire telegraph pole, black, with four arms. Pole on round base. Later called TP4 (1952).

TPD Telegraph Pole   1. 1950,1952. Quite scarce.
See TD6.

TP1 Telegraph Pole with base   1950. 11d. Quite scarce.
Four arm pole made and advertised by Don Bowles. Became BJ Ward's TPB.

TP4 Telegraph Pole   1. 1952,1957. 5d each. Quite scarce.
See TP.

TPB4 Telegraph Pole   1. 1952,1957. 8d, 1/-. Quite scarce.
See TPB.

TPD6 Telegraph Pole   1. 1952,1957. 10d. Quite scarce.
See TD6.

WB4 Wagon Buffers   4. 1953. 9d. Scarce in packet.

WC Water Crane   1. 1950,1953. 2/6, 3/4. Scarce.
Water crane (grey) with hose (black) and chain. Water valve winding handle on base. (See No 48) A Don Bowles design.

Water Towers

T Water Tower   1. 1950. 4/11. Scarce.

Called a water tower, but later called a column.
A Don Bowles design.

TH Water Tower   1. 1951. 6/9. Scarce.
This is a water tower (column) with a hut on the base.
A Don Bowles design.

TNL Water Tower   1. 1951,1952. 6/1. Scarce.
This is a water tower (column) with a ladder, two hoses and chains. I suggest the 'L' in TNL stands for large, so as to be used trackside.
A Don Bowles design which is 3 ½" high.

TNS Water Tower   1. 1951. 6/1½ Scarce.
This is a water tower (column) without a ladder, but has two hoses and chains. I suggest the 'S' in TNS stands for short, as these towers are quite small and suitable to be platform mounted.
A Don Bowles design. All same height at 2 $^{5}/_{8}$".

The one on the left is W.T.A. in 1950

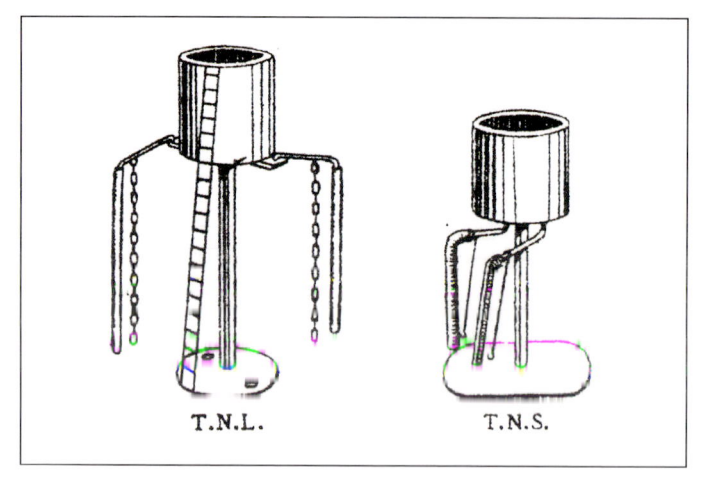

Extract from Bradshaws November 1952
Catalogue with the above two towers compared.

WT Water Tower   1. 1951,1953. 6/6. Scarce with box or wrapped in brown paper.

Water tank (grey) on steel girder frame (grey).

Note the address on the box. See Chapter Three on BJ Ward.

Became WT1 in 1955.

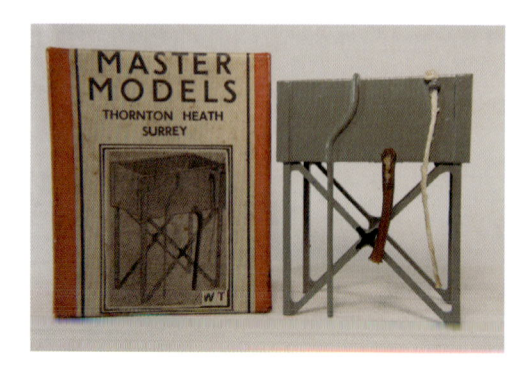

WT1 Water Tower   1. 1955,1957. Scarce in either box.
Renumbering of WT but with different packaging.

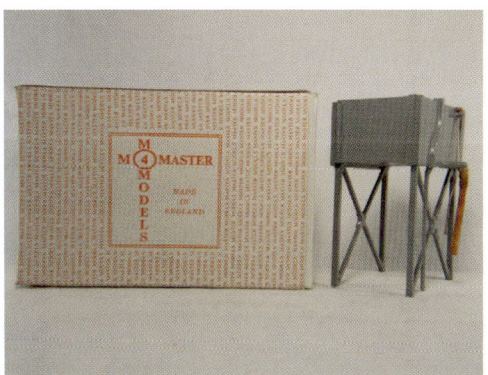

WT2 Water Tower   1. 1953,1955. 6/-. Scarce, with or without box.
Cast water tank on building. Building made of wood and covered in brick paper.
Two different designs on building known.

WT4 Water Tower, Platform Mounted   1. 1950. 6/3.
The original water tower reclassified by BJ Ward as TNB. See TNS and picture on left hand side.

Other Wardie Items
The following listings are non Kemlows and Don Bowles, but appear in the MasterModel listings over the years.

BBS/1 Bridge End Supports   2. 1956. 4/11, 5/11. Scarce.
Wood and cardboard embankment ends (green mottled with red and yellow splashes) to support single girder bridge No 68. Wrapped in brown paper.

BBS/2 Bridge End Supports   2. 1956. Scarce.
As BBS/1 but for double girder bridge No 77. Wrapped in brown paper.

Posters

These are mainly railway posters available in cellophane packets stapled to shop display cards. These cards have a fluorescent MasterModel motif and "MINIATURE POSTERS AND SIGNS" in bright red and green on black background.

TT-Gauge Posters and Signs   100. 1955.

1/-1/2. Scarce on card.

Similar to 00 variety. States 2-3mm on card.

D3 Sheet of Miniature Posters (00)   12. 1955. Scarce on card.

00 Posters, Packets of 25   1955,1960. Scarce.

Railway posters. Also available in 0 and TT scales.

00 Posters, Packets of 50   1955,1959. Scarce on card.

Railway posters. Also available in 0 and TT scales.

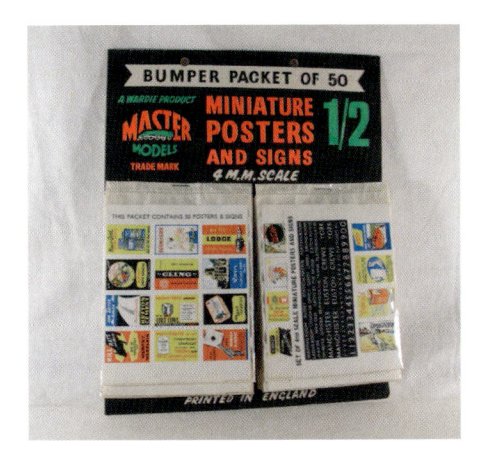

00 Posters, Packets of 80   1955, 1960.
Scarce on card.
As above.

00 Posters, Packets of 80   Scarce on card.
As above but on foolscap sheets advertising garage posters.

0 Posters, Packets of 50   Scarce on card.
As 00 packets of 50, but 7mm scale.

0 Garage Posters, Packets of 80   Scarce on card.
Packets of garage posters. Stapled onto original MasterModels shop card. Early 1960s.

Garage Posters   Scarce on card.
Printed by JNT Model Products Ltd. Shop card with stapled packets of posters. Not identified as Wardie, but has K.90 in the top left hand corner, which suggests BJ Ward K Series in 1960s.

00 Scale Scenic Background
4. 1953,1961.   Quite common.
Four different scenic background sheets, 20" x 8".
Became No 98 in 1961.

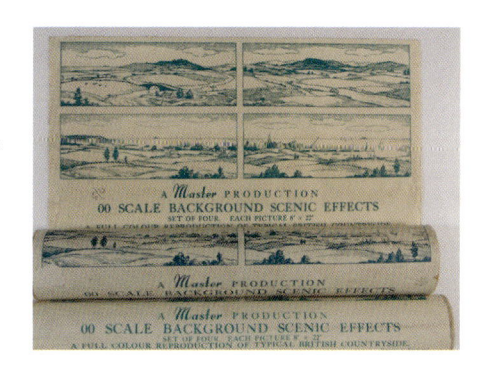

Imitation Grass Mat   1. 1958,1960. Very scarce in wrap.
22" x 12" mat with suede finish.

Pure Rayon Flock   1. Very scarce in wrap.
Packet of rayon flock. Green or brown.

Signal Arms   1953. Very scarce.
Upper and lower quadrant signal arms.

Scale Town Buildings

Because of the simplicity of these buildings i.e. blocks of wood, or ply with paper décor or paint, they were not seen as quality items. Consequently, not many have survived over the years.

This makes them very rare and collectable these days. These buildings appeared as MasterModels to be mainly used as background or low relief, thus lacked detail. Some, though, are quite fine (e.g. *BR7*).

BR/1 Dog and Partridge Inn   1953. 21/-. Scarce.

BR/2 Black Horse Inn   1953. 21/-. Scarce.

BR/3 Tudor House   1953. 14/6. Scarce.

BR/4 Blue Anchor Inn   1953. 21/- Scarce

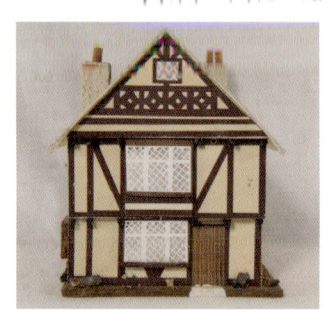

THE MASTER MODEL RANGE

BR7 Transformer Station   1953,1956. 5/6. Scarce.

Made from blocks of wood, hardboard, brick paper. Panel pins and cotton for fence. Quite a complex model. Two different models shown.

BR/8 House   1954,1957. 6/-. Scarce.

THE KEMLOW STORY

BR/9 Barber Shop 1954, 1955. 6/-. Scarce.

BR/10 The Rising Sun 1954, 1957. 6/6. Scarce.

THE MASTER MODEL RANGE   77

BR/11 The Bell Inn   1954,1955. 6/6. Scarce.

BR/12 The Coach Inn   1954,1957. 6/11. Scarce.

BR/13 The Smuggler's Inn   1954,1956. 6/11. Scarce.

BR/14 Royal Hotel   1954,1956. 7/6. Scarce.

BR/15 Antique Shoppe   1954,1957. 7/6. Scarce.

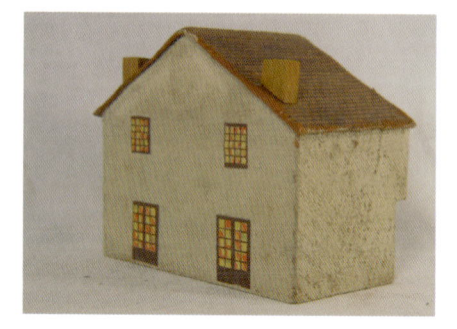

BR/16 Corner Shop   1954,1955. 7/6. Scarce.

BR/17 Manor House   1954,1955.   7/11.   Scarce.

MS/1 Office Building   1955.   9/6.   Very scarce.

Four storey modern building. Low profile. Made of ply with stencilled paintwork.

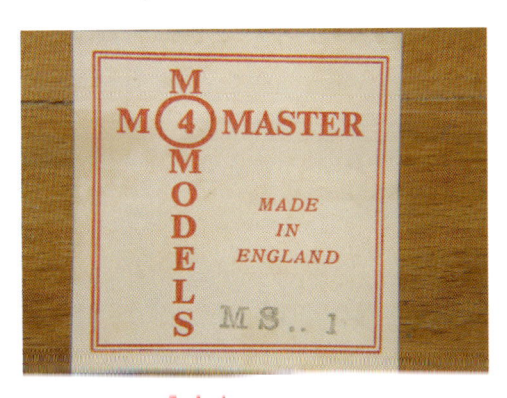

Label on reverse

MS/2 Hospital Building   1955.   9/6.   Very scarce.

Two storey modern building. Low profile. Made of ply with stencilled paintwork.

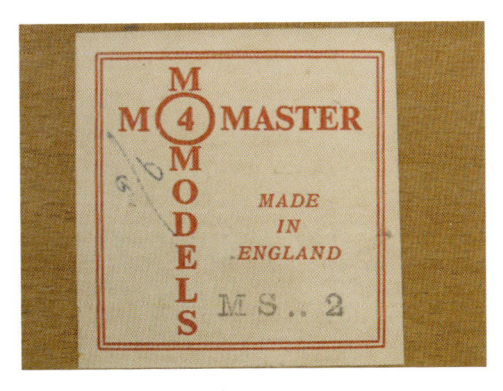

Label on reverse

MS/3 Flats   1955. 9/6. Very scarce.

Four storey modern building. Low profile. Made of ply with stencilled paintwork.

TS/1 The Coach Inn   1955. 6/-. Very scarce.

Low profile, plywood construction.

TS/2 The Rising Sun   1955. 7/-. Very scarce.

Low profile, plywood construction.

TS/3 Antique Shoppe   1955. 6/-. Very scarce.

Low profile, plywood construction.

Reverse

TS/4 Tea Shop & Barbers   1955. 7/-. Very scarce.

Low profile, plywood construction.

Reverse

TS/5 House   1955. 7/6. Very scarce.

Low profile, plywood construction.

MasterModels Numbered Sets Listing

Special Value Sets 1, 2 and 3

1. Presentation Set of 8 MasterModels   8. 1952, deleted 1955. 6/-. Scarce. Buffer stop (from BS1), timetable (from T3), hoarding (from H3), four track signs (from BC4) and a seat (from SG).

2. Presentation Set of 7 MasterModels   7. 1952, deleted 1955. 6/-. Scarce. Sidings buffer (from BS2), two track signs (from BC4), two station lamps with adverts (LSA), timetable (T3) and a seat (SG).

3. Presentation Set of 8 MasterModels   8. 1952, deleted 1955. 6/-. Scarce. Two timetables (T1&T3), four track signs (BC4) and two hoardings (H2&H3).

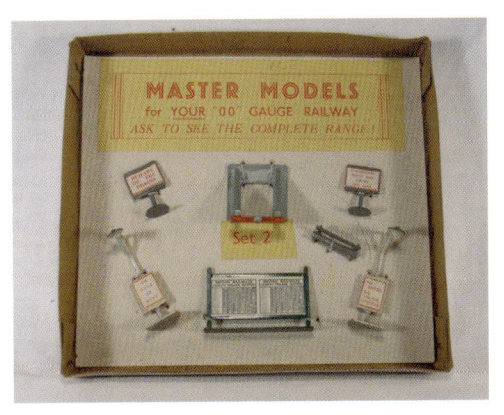

1. Track Accessories   4. 1950K, deleted 1953. 2/-, 2/6. Quite scarce.
Telegraph pole (brown, 3 arm). Level sign (brown/white). Station name hoarding (green). Lamp standard (green).

1. Railway Staff   6. 1950K, deleted 1960. 2/-, 2/6.
Earlier set (quite scarce): Porter (dark blue) with bag on shoulder and bag in hand.
Porter (dark blue) with sack barrow (brown).
Guard (dark blue) with lowered flag.
Porter (dark blue) carrying silver box.
Station Master (dark blue).
Later set (quite common): As above, but last two pieces are replaced by
Porter (dark blue) carrying two cases by side.
Guard (dark blue) carrying lamp aloft.

Earlier sets

THE MASTER MODEL RANGE   83

Later sets

2. *Railway Passengers*   5. 1951K,1960. 2/-, 2/6. Common.

Man (grey) carrying umbrella in right hand. Postman (dark blue) carrying letter and post bag. Man (green or brown) carrying golf clubs. Woman in suit (blue or cream). Boy (blue or yellow) or girl (red or yellow) or woman in orange pleated dress (later sets).

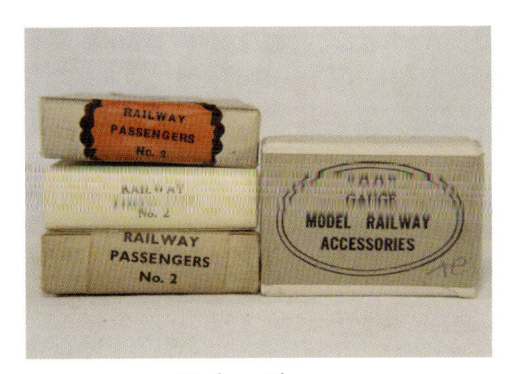

Early set boxes    Early set

Later set    Later set

*3. **Assorted Figures** 5. 1951K,1960. 2/-, 2/6. Common.

Man (green) with umbrella in left hand. Man in evening suit (black). Woman in coat (cream or red or green). Woman in long dress (white) and cape (blue). Boy or girl (as in Set 2).

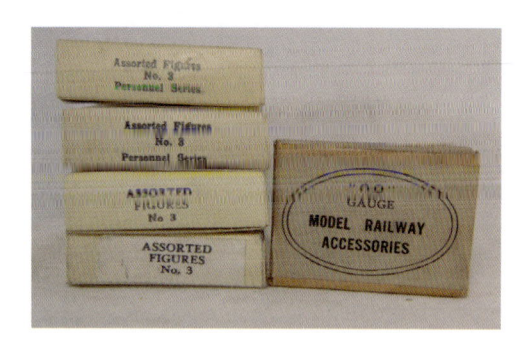

*4. **Seated Passengers** 5. 1951K,1960. 2/-, 2/6. Common.

WREN (navy blue). Two soldiers (khaki uniforms). Woman in coat (yellow or green). Man in boiler suit (red).

Seat not included

*5. **Seated Passengers** 4. 1951K,1962. 2/-, 2/6. Common.

Courting couple as one piece (man red or cream, woman cream and blue). Holy Sister (black and white). Man in coat (pink or cream or brown). Woman in coat (blue or cream).

THE MASTER MODEL RANGE   85

Seat not included

6. *Double Station Seat*   2. 1951K,1960. 2/-. Common.

Pairs of double back to back seats (grey or dark brown or rust brown or mid green or dark green).

7. *Platform Accessories*   7. 1951K,1960. 2/-, 2/6. Common.

Weighing machine (pink or cream). Fry's chocolate machine (red). Three $3/8''$ milk churns. Bicycle (assorted colours). Platform trolley (blue or green). A clock from Set 66 is found in addition in the stapled packets.

86   THE KEMLOW STORY

8. Milk Churns   12. 1951K,1961. 1/6. Common.

$3/8''$ (as in Set 7) or $1/2''$ or $1/2''$ plated (1958) or $7/16''$ plated (1958).

Most common 1951

1958   1958   1958

9.. Single Track Level Crossing Gates   2. 1951K,1961.
2/6, 3/-. Common.

Just one pair of gates. Two sets would be required for complete crossing. White with red discs. Supporting wire from post to gate. Red lamp on gate. Dark, mid or lime green post base.

Earlier Don Bowles sets called LCG (1951) had no supporting wire or red lamp.

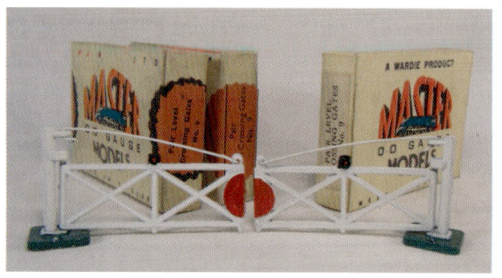

Earlier set   Later set

THE MASTER MODEL RANGE

10. Platform Equipment   4.   1951K,1966.   2/-, 2/6.   Common.

Metal lamp (green single in early sets. Green or mushroom double in later sets). Bus or coach stop (cream). Telephone kiosk (red). Oval or round pillar box (red).

Early set

Later sets

Stapled packet

This cost is an extra item in the stapled packet

11. Sheep in Pen   5.   1958,1960.   2/6.   Quite scarce.

Four sheep (grey, Britain's Lilliput) on a wooden base (grey or green) pen. Enclosure is metal fencing (green or fawn) with a gate. Note: K56 (from the Kemlows 'K' series) is an identical set with fawn fencing.

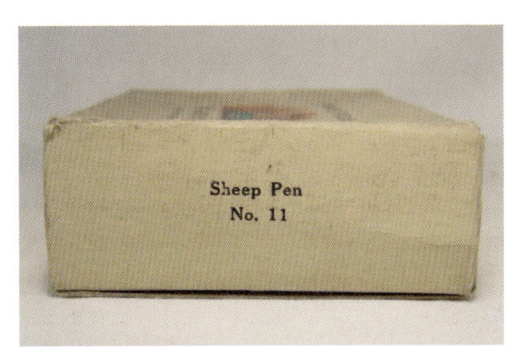

88   THE KEMLOW STORY

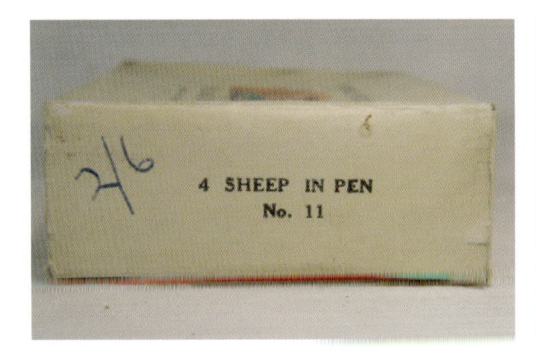

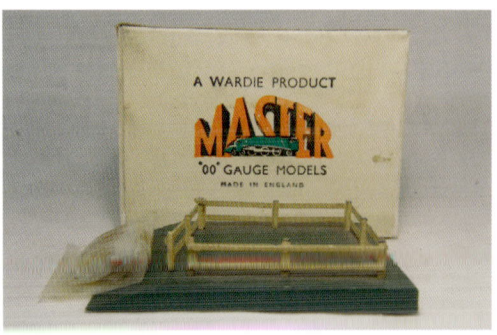

11. Gradient Posts   6. 1951K,1955. Scarce in box.
Brown with white arms.

12. Electric Trolley and Trailer   7. 1951K,1959. 2/6, 1/9. Common.
Station trolley (blue) and trailer (blue). Driver (dark blue - pins on feet fit into holes at front of trolley). Two barrels (grey or brown). Two small wooden crates (cream). Barrels and drums same as Britain's Lilliput.

13. Not used.

14. W H Smith Kiosk   1. 1951K, 1962. 4/6, 5/-. Common.

Double sided. Dark green, mid green or lime green. Very popular casting. Quite easy to find.

15. Telephone Kiosk   2. 1951K, 1956. 2/-. Common.

Red, with red and white paper wrap.

15. Police and Telephone Kiosks   2. 1956, 1959. 2/-. Quite common.

A later set 15 combining the earlier Set 15 and Set 24.

Police box, dark blue with blue and white paper wrap. Telephone box, with red and white paper wrap.

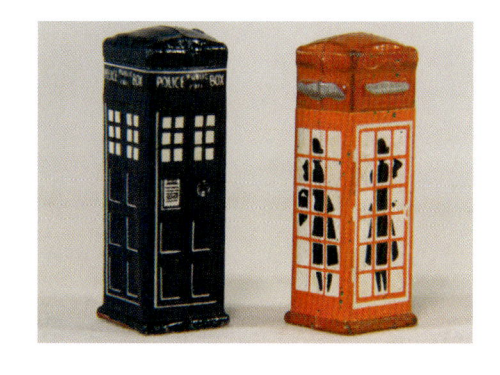

16. Station Lamps   3. 1952K,1961 or 1958,1961. 2/6. Common.

Either three metal (mushroom and green) as in Set 10 OR three concrete lamps (cream or white) introduced in 1958.

Earlier metal lamps

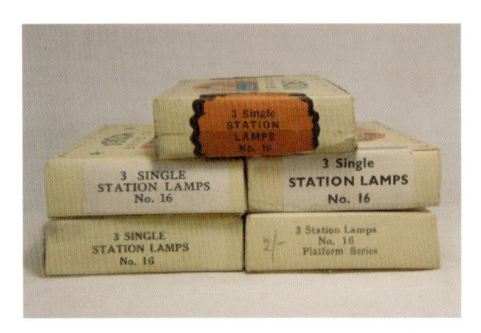

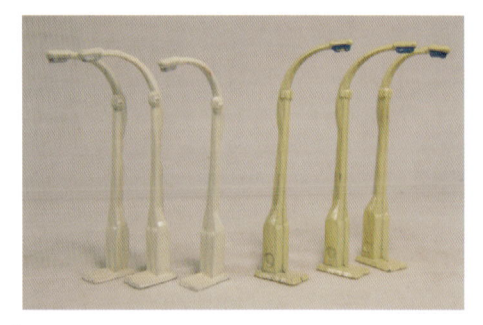

Later concrete lamps

17. Steel Girders   6. 1951K. 1/6. Very scarce in box.

Unpainted steel girders (grey). 1 5/8" long.

Only ever advertised twice: 1. Model Railway News, March 1952.
2. Bradshaws Cat. 1953/4 as F1 - Freight Series No 1.

In the top 5 for scarcity. Due to its unattractiveness, I suspect few sold.

THE MASTER MODEL RANGE 91

*18. **Cable Holders (Unlagged)***   2. 1951K,1958. 2/-. Common.
Two black (all diecast) drums with silver cable. Henley labels attached.

A rare set. Freight Series No 2 in early box

*18. **Cable Drums***   2. 1955,1958. 2/-.
One lagged (brown), one unlagged (black) cable drums. Henley labels attached. In 1958 cardboard ends were introduced to both lagged and unlagged drums. Not common.

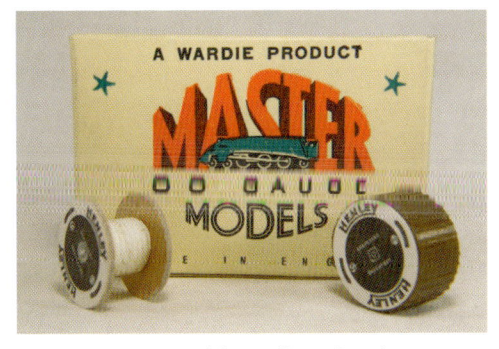

Common   Drums with cardboard ends

*19. **Tar Barrels***   6. 1951K,1957. 1/-, 1/3. Common.
Small black barrels with painted yellow ends.

19. Tar and Oil Barrels
2x6. 1951K,1957. 2/6. Common.
Six tar barrels (as above) and six oil barrels (as in Set 20).

19/20. Oil and Tar Barrels
2x6. 1958,1961. 2/6. Common.
As above set but released later.

20. Oil Barrels
6. 1951K,1957. 1/-, 1/3. Common.
Small grey barrels with painted white ends.

21. Platform Gardens, Island Type
2. 1952K,1957. 1/3, 1/6. Quite common.
One rectangular flower bed (black with white edging) with four plants and a bush. One diamond flower bed (black with white edging) with four plants and a bush.

21/22. Platform Gardens, Island and Wall Type

4. 1958,1959. 2/-. Quite scarce. Combined set of Sets 21 and 22.

22. Platform Gardens, Wall Type

2. 1952K,1957. 1/3, 1/6. Quite common. Two part round wall gardens (black with white edging) with three plants and two bushes.

23. Track Repair Party

6. 1952K,1960. 2/-, 2/6. Common.
Man (black and brown) waving flag (red or green). Man (grey) with shovel. Man (grey) with sledge hammer. Man (black and brown or green) with pick axe. Man (grey) with wheelbarrow (brown or grey or green or red).

A set has been seen where all the men are wearing black trousers.

24. Police Boxes   2. 1952K,1958. 2/-. Common.

Two dark blue boxes with white and blue paper wrap. Rounded (most common), stepped and flat roofed boxes exist.

25. Placards   3. 1952K,1957. 1/3, 1/6. Quite scarce.

Three posters on three boards. Boards in green or black or grey or cream. Only two different posters seen.

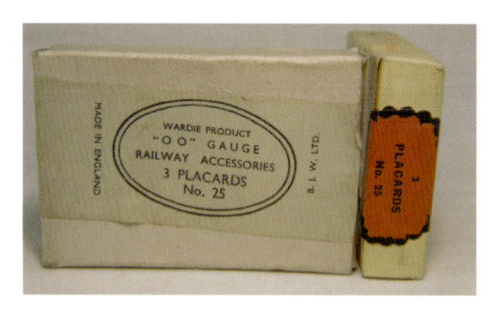

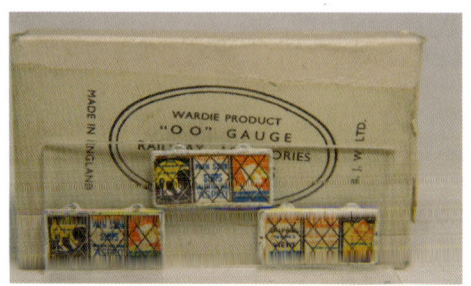

26. Sleeper Buffer   1. 1952K,1960. 2/-, 2/6. Common.

Box shaped bin made of sleepers (dark green, lime green, or black) and filled with sand or ballast, supporting a red beam.

Note: Similar casts marked S-R inside (for Stuart Redpath) are sometimes mistaken for the MasterModel one.

27. Scales with Light Goods   5. 1952,1957. 1/-. Very scarce.

Platform weighing scales (green or black). Basket (yellow) with fruit (red). Golf bag (green or brown). Suitcase (brown). Ladies suitcase (blue or black). Due to the small numbers made and the size of these items, I consider these to be perhaps the rarest MasterModels set.

Rarest set

28. Signal Ladders   6. 1953,1959. 4d each ladder, 2/- the card.

A card is scarce. Six tin plated steel ladders, 5 inches long, mounted on shop display backing card. Two brown, two green and two black.

29. Glass Crates   3. 1952,1959. 1/-. Uncommon.

Three cast crates (cream or brown) in paper wraps to depict planking and labels.

30. Corrugated Iron Sheets   3. 1953,1958. 1/-. Common.

Three corrugated iron sheets. Usually unpainted pressed steel (not tin foil).

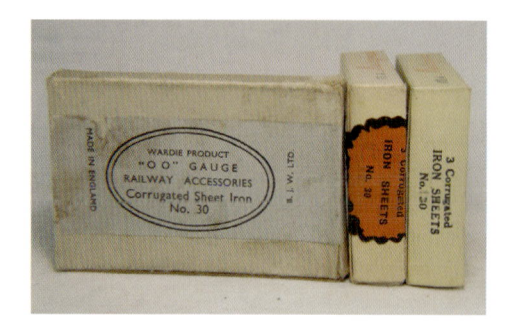

31. Enquiry Kiosks   2. 1952K,1958. 2/-. Common.

Two enquiry kiosks (green) in white and green wrap to depict kiosk. Man in kiosk is depicted. Rounded (most common) and stepped roofs exist. Flat roofs do exist as well with a casting flash in the middle of the roof, but are usually found in the later set, no.88.

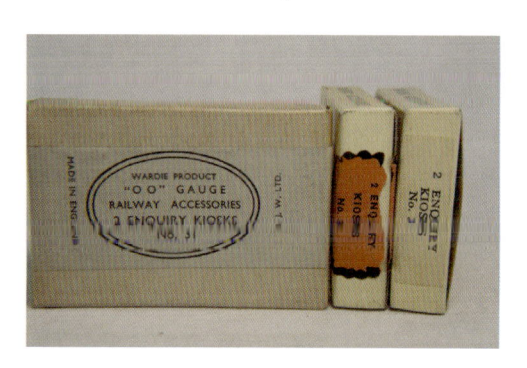

THE MASTER MODEL RANGE

32. Henley Lagged Cable Drums 2. 1952,1957. 2/-. Common.

Two lagged cable drums (brown) as in Sets 18 and 35.

33. Esso Oil Drums 3. 1952,1953. 1/3. Uncommon in box.

Three drums (red) with printed Esso labels (red and white). Only put in boxes of three for one year, thus rare packaging. Oil drums are quite common from the set 33 that follows. The blue box wrap is unique and only found with this set.

33. Esso Oil Drums 6. 1955,1961. 2/6. Common.

Three drums (red) with printed Esso labels (red and white). Three drums (green) with printed Esso labels (red and white).

Various shades of green seen

34. Watchman's Hut   2. 1952,1960. 2/6, 3/-. Common.

Sentry type hut (black, but red has been seen) on base (different shades of grey or different shades of green) with braziers (tin foil as fire). Man (grey) with sledge hammer.

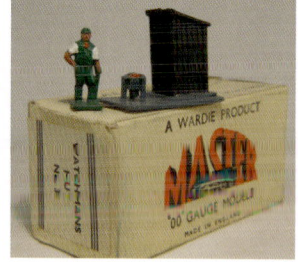

A rare red hut

35. Cable Laying Party   5. 1952,1962. 2/6, 3/-. Common.

Lagged or unlagged cable drum (see sets 18 and 32). Man (grey) with sledgehammer. Man (brown and black) with pick axe. Man (grey) with wheelbarrow (grey or brown or green or red).

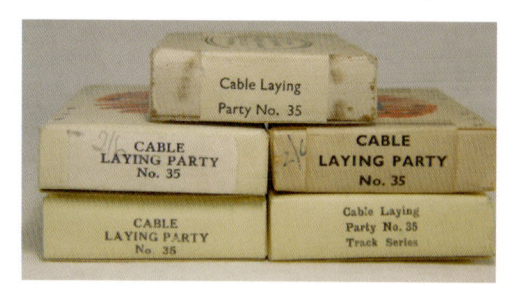

36. Finlay's Tobacco Stall   1. 1952,1962. 4/6, 5/-. Quite scarce.

Same casting as No 14 W H Smith Kiosk but with tobacco posters. Less common than the W H Smith Kiosk. A range of colours have been seen, i.e. mid brown (matt), brown/red (gloss), dark brown (gloss), dark pink (matt), pink (matt). Two sets of posters have been seen.

Unopened examples

THE MASTER MODEL RANGE

Common type of posters

Rare example of posters

37. Walton's Fruit Stall   1. 1952, 1962. 4/6, 5/-. Quite scarce.
Same casting as No 14 W H Smith Kiosk, but with fruit stall posters. Less common than the W H Smith. Only two colours exist, gloss black and matt black.

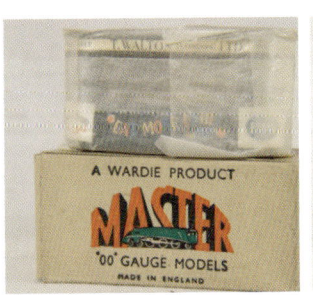

Unopened example

38. Sand Bin and Fire Buckets   3. 1952, 1961. 2/-, 2/6. Common.
Semi cylindrical sand bin (with red paper wrap). Four buckets mounted on rack (red). Man (grey) with shovel. Bin and buckets can be separate, or mounted on red card.

Separate pieces

Mounted on card

39. Station Names and Seat   1. 1952,1957. 2/-, 2/6. Common.

Cream or mushroom or grey name boards attached to green or cream seat. Came with two named labels, but assorted packets have been found in some boxes. The following names have been seen: Glasgow, Waterloo, Swansea, Edinburgh, Crewe, Trugage Halt, Truegauge Halt (red letters) and Masterhalt. These are a different design from those in Set 60. A range of different boxes were used.

Packet of assorted names   Selection of seats

40. Permanent Way Cabin   2. 1952,1960. 4/8, 5/-. Common.

Hut (black) with chimney stack at rear, on base (green or dark brown or rust or grey). Man (grey) with shovel or man (brown and black) with pick axe. Barrel to take rainwater (red or green or grey or silver). This set is called a Platelayers Hut in some catalogues.

41. Water Column   1. 1953,1960. 2/6, 3/-. Common.

Single column on round base (brown or red oxide or grey or green) with ladder and single hose. Two different swivel hose mechanisms exist. One cast, the other wire. Earlier versions of this column were Don Bowles designs and called Water Towers (T, TH, TNL or TNS).

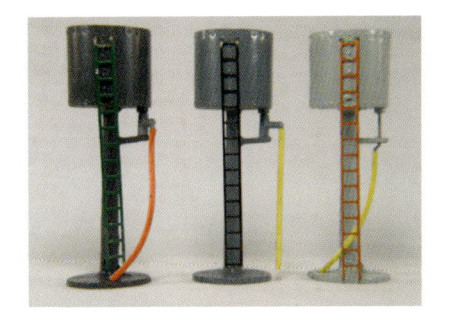

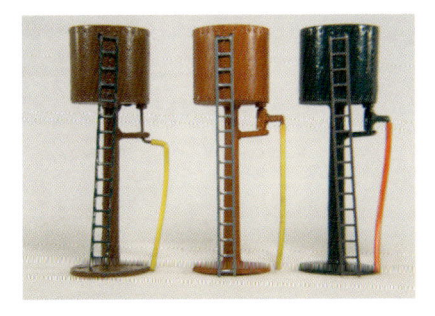

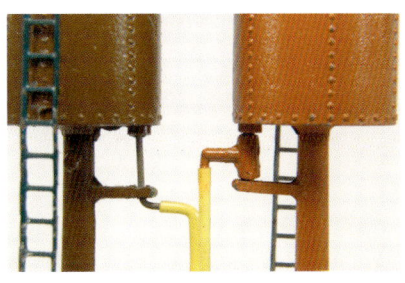

Different hose mechanism

42. Railway Container   1. 1953, 1961. 1/6, 2/6. Rare in box.
Container (green or grey) with "Carter Patterson" label (mid or dark green). This is identical to the Trix version and opens up the possibility that Kemlows cast these for Trix as well as BJ Ward.
OR container (green or grey) with "Smiths Bluecol" label (mid or dark green) OR container (grey) with "British Railways Furniture" paper wrap (brown).

43. Cycles and Rack   5. 1952,1960. 2/-, 2/6. Common.

Cycle rack (grey) with slots to slot tyres into, with four cycles (blue, green, yellow or red, any combination.)

44. Petrol Pumps   2. 1952,1957. 2/-. Uncommon.

Pair of pumps (red or blue pairs) with Esso labels. Larger than '00'. Same castings used for green pumps in K16 Filling Station. See later.

45. Coal Office   1. 1953,1960. 4/-. Common.

Coal office (various shades of grey) with green door (various shades) or brown door (various shades). This is the same casting as No 40 Permanent Way Cabin with name board fitted to roof. Base plate (and so barrel) not used.

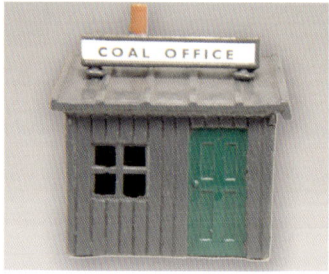

46. Not used.

47. Not used.

*48. **Water Crane** 1. 1953,1961. 2/-. Common.*
Water crane (dark brown or green or grey) with plastic hose (black). This is identical to the Hornby Dublo casting, but with MASTER MODELS cast on underside of base. This is the only MasterModel with this mark. This raises the question of whether Kemlows cast the Hornby ones with a similar die and BJ Ward insisting on his MasterModels die having its own mark. Stephen Lowe recalls subcontracting for Meccano.

*49. **Level Crossing Gates** 1. 1953,1961. 8/9, 9/-. Common.*
Gates (white) on base (two grey pieces bolted together). Gates supported by wire from post. Red warning discs and red gate lamps.

a) Earlier type has single posts and no gate lugs.

b) Later type has double posts and gate lugs.

c) 1958, third type, called "Level Crossing Gates on Ramp" has cast or tin plate ramps as two separate pieces to allow for adjustable width between track(s). Not so common.

Earlier set. Single posts. No gate lugs    Later set. Double posts. Gate lugs

Cast ramps  · Tin plate ramps

50. AA Box, Patrolman and Motorcycle   3. 1953,1960. 2/6, 3/-. Common.
Classic AA motorcycle and sidecar (yellow and black). A separate mounted patrolman (khaki uniform). Some motorcycles and sidecars are fixed together, others plug in as separate pieces. Plastic and metal wheels have been seen.
AA box has No 54 printed (Colchester - Clacton road). See Set 61. This site was a stopping point for the Lowes on family days out.

51. Semaphore Ground Signals   2. 1953,1957. 3/6. Uncommon.
Ground signal (black) with arm (grey or red or yellow). Spring lever mechanism. Some have been found to have plastic jewels to represent lights. S&B made similar signals which are more common. Look for S&B diamond on base.

51/52. Ground Signals

2. 1958,1959. 3/6. Scarce.
A semaphore ground signal (Set 51) and a disc shunting signal (Set 52). S&B produced a similar, more common, disc shunting signal.

52. Disc Shunting Signal

2. 1953,1957. 3/6. Scarce.
S&B made a similar, more common signal. Again, look for the S&B mark on the base.

53. Four Aspect Searchlight Junction Signal

2. 1953,1957. 3/6. Uncommon.
Junction signal (black) with ladder. Dummy lights.

Front and back views

54. Two Arm Electric Banner Signal

2. 1953,1957. 3/-. Uncommon.
Banner Signal (black) with ladder. Two round discs (grey, one with red strip and other green) on horizontal banner.

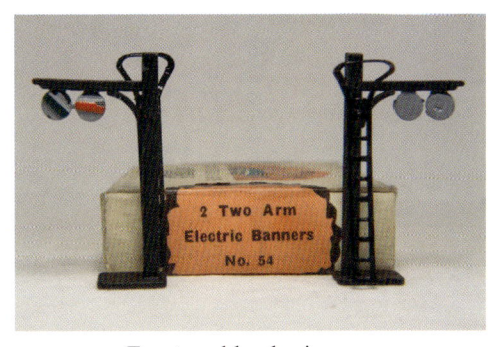

Front and back views

55. Three Aspect Colour Signals
2. 1953,1957. 3/-. Uncommon.
Colour light signal (black) with ladder.
Dummy lights (red, yellow and green)
on grey background plate.

Front and back views

56. Single Aspect Searchlight Signal
2. 1953,1957. 2/9. Uncommon.
Single aspect signal (black) with
ladder. Dummy light (green) on grey
surround.

Front and back views

57. Crew Unloading Truck   7. 1953,1960. 2/6, 3/-. Common.
Man in dungarees (cream) with arm raised to carry plank. Man in dungarees (brown) with arm raised to carry plank. Plank is size and shape of matchstick. Man in dungarees (light blue) supporting box (brown) on head. Man in dungarees (light blue) carrying box (brown) in front. Man (black and grey) with arms raised directing operations. Foreman in suit (black) and bowler hat.

58. Track Ballast   Packet. 1953,1961. 1/6. Very scarce in packet.
A packet of '00' gauge track ballast. As yet unseen.

59. Tarpaulin Covers   2. 1953,1961. 2/-. Common.
Tarpaulin sheets (black cotton) with white cross (BR 317521). Ropes from the four corners. Not to be confused with those made for Trix wagons.

60. Station Names   Packet of 12. 1953,1957. 3/6. Uncommon.
Six pairs of different station names (on coloured backgrounds) on gummed paper. The packet has printed on it "A WARDIE PRODUCT. STATION NAMES. NO 60".

Packet with contents   Contents

61. AA Boxes

2. 1953,1961. 2/6. Common.

Two of the AA boxes as found in Set 50. The box has a silver roof and paper wrap depicting Box 54. This actual box was on the Colchester-Clacton road.

62. Police Cycle Patrolman and Box 3. 1953,1961. 2/-, 2/6. Uncommon.

Police box (dark blue) with white and blue paper wrap. Police motor cycle (matt or gloss red oxide or gloss black). This is a repaint of the AA bike from Set 50. It is similar to the Britain's Lilliput bike, but smaller.

The police rider is a separate piece and again a repaint of the AA riders from Set 50. Note: the names on the box packaging vary.

Various titles

Matt red oxide bike  Gloss red oxide bike  Gloss black bike

63. Oval Pillar Boxes 2. 1953,1957. 1/6. Common.

Two oval pillar boxes. Red with black base or red with black base and top.

Black base  Black base and top

64. Wicket Gate   1. 1953,1960. 2/6, 2/9. Common.

This was called a kissing gate by the Lowes. Gate (white or grey) with fencing rails (green or black) on base (green or black). Fences were separate and slotted into lugs in base.

Whilst this gate is boxed as '00' gauge, it is out of scale and larger. Difficult to fit onto your '00' layout.

William Lowe sketched this gate situated next to a branch line from St. Margaret's station to Ware (north out of Liverpool St) often visited by the Lowe family.

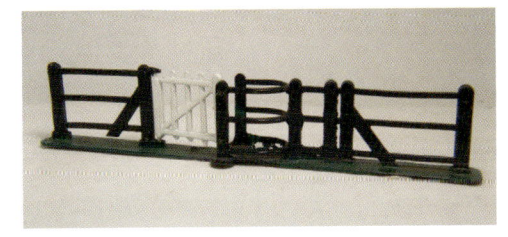

Usual colours

Original site in 2008. The rail track was just beyond the replacement stile. The two vertical steel posts at either end are what remains of the original fence

65. Charrington's Coal Bunker   3. 1954,1960. 4/-. Common.

Coal bunker (grey) with sign board "Coal CHARRINGTONS Coke". Coal man (brown and black) carrying sack of coal. Rare as only found with this set.

Scales (as in Set 27). Coal is sometimes cemented into bunker. Otherwise, supplied in packet.

Just the coal staithes are very common.

66. Two Station Clocks

2. 1954,1961. 1/-, 1/6. Uncommon.

Two double sided station clocks (green or blue) with paper dial (white or yellow). Ideal to tack onto Woodside Stations (or any other '00' gauge stations) via the holes in the mounting brackets.

67. Street Personnel

5. 1954,1957. 2/-, 2/6. Common.

Women in coat (yellow). Newspaper seller (green). Kneeling boot boy (red and black) cleaning shoes of man (grey and black). Separate pieces. Policeman directing traffic (dark blue uniform).

The woman was sometimes omitted from this set.

67/69. Street Personnel

8. 1956,1962. 2/6, 3/-. Common.

Combined set of Set 67 and Set 69.

THE MASTER MODEL RANGE

68. Single Girder Bridge   1. 1954,1962. 10/9, 11/-. Common.

Single hogsback type girder bridge. Seen in light grey, mid grey, dark grey, light and dark red oxide.

Stephen Lowe of Kemlows suggests that from a casting point of view, this was the best model they made (along with perhaps the Guy Pickfords Van - not in this range).

See comments on no.77, Double Girder Bridge.

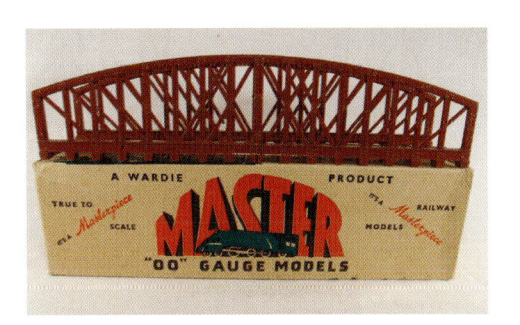

69. Belisha Crossing Set

3. 1954,1957. 1/6. Uncommon.

Crossing patrol woman (white) holding 'stop' sign (all one piece). Two Belisha beacons (black/white, orange globe).

70. London Transport Bus Shelter 1. 1955,1960. 2/6. Common.

London Transport bus shelter (dark, mid or lime grey). Double-sided, with London transport posters.

71. Goods Yard Crane   2. 1955,1962. 8/9, 10/6. Scarce in box.

Crane (grey or beige) that swivels on a separate base (dark grey). Jib is supported by two wires. A ratchet handle winds up a hook via string.

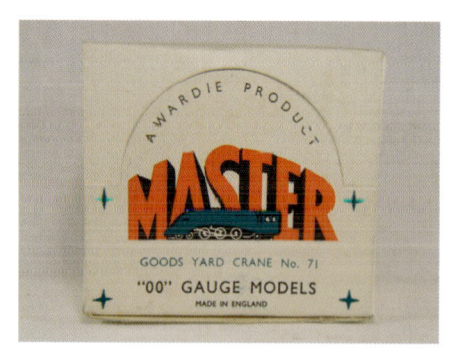

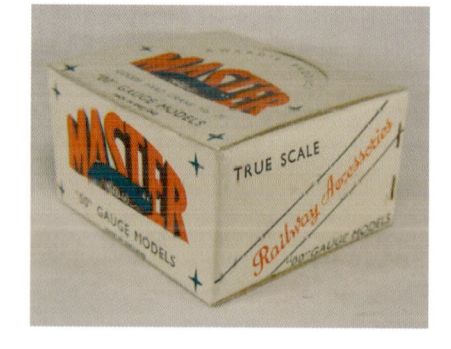

Counter display box

72. Gent's Toilet   2. 1954,1961. 4/6. Common.

Old fashioned open urinal (light or dark green). Two separate pieces, sometimes mounted on thin black card.

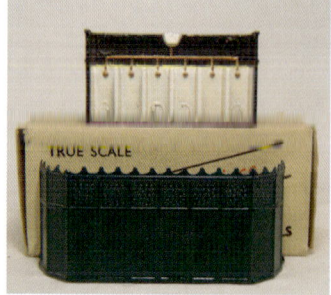

Mounted on black card   As separate pieces

THE MASTER MODEL RANGE

73. Mine Workers 6. 1955,1957. 2/-, 2/6. Scarce.

Man (black boiler suit) with shovel. Man (black boiler suit) with pickaxe. Man (black boiler suit) with sledgehammer. Man (black boiler suit) with wheelbarrow (grey). Man (black) with raised arm blowing whistle. All figures have silver knee pads and silver hat lamps. These figures appear in Set 23 and Set 35, and so arc repaints of these previous sets.

In the 1957 MasterModels Catalogue-Handbook, the man with arm raised is replaced by another man with pickaxe.

Stephen Lowe of Kemlows says that this set is not surprising as the man in charge of the paint shop at Kemlows had relatives in the Welsh mines. Not an obvious railway accessory, so rare to find.

74. One Dozen Fences 12. 1955,1960. 6d each, 6d pair. Scarce in box.

A box of 12 6-inch railway type fences (lime green, or mid green, or dark green, or white, which is rare). Same railing as used on Set 89.

Difficult to find in a complete box as usually sold individually.

Box usually has rust marks as railings are a very tight fit and score the box.

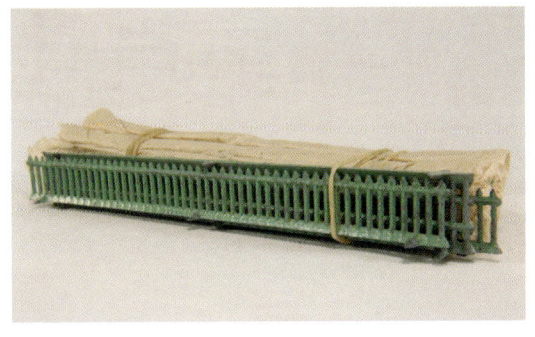

75 Seat with Figures   4. 1955,1959. 2/6. Quite common.

A single grey seat (from set SG or SG4) or single green seat (from set SM or SM4) or a double station seat (from Set 6).

Three seated passengers. Type appears to be random.

Set with single seat

Set with double seat

Top right box is from set below

75. Station Name and Seat with Figures   4. 1953,1959. 2/6. Quite common.

Station name and seat (as Set 39) with three seated figures (type appears to be random), or double green seat (as set 6) with three seated figures.

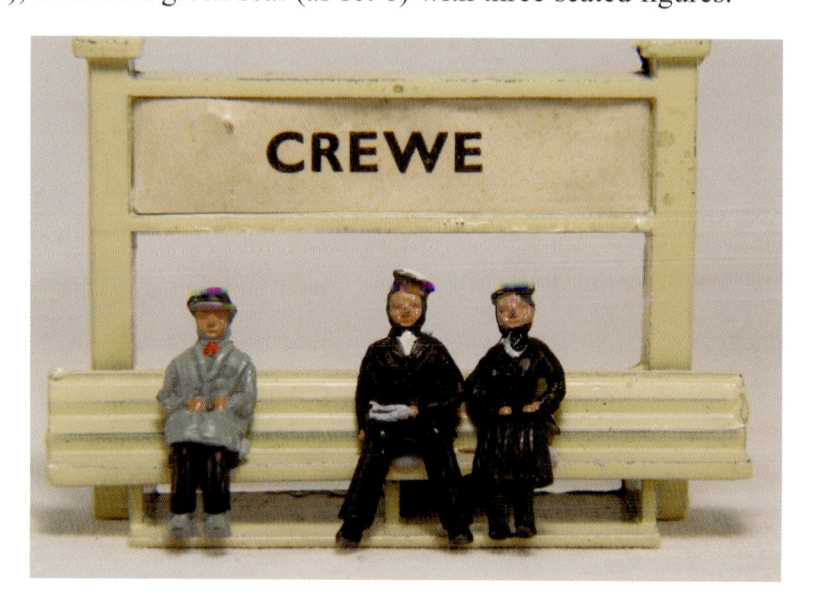

*76. **Double Track Crossing Gates**   2. 1955,1961. 3/9, 3/10. Quite common.
Just one pair of gates (white) with posts into green base. Support wires with lamp and red warning disc.
Two sets would be needed for complete crossing.

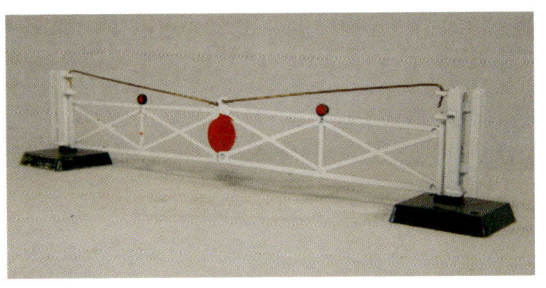

*77. **Double Girder Bridge**   1. 1955,1960. 12/6, 12/11. Uncommon.
Double hogsback type girder bridge (light and dark grey only) made from compressing together two single girder bridges (Set 68) via a central support. Again, this is considered by Stephen Lowe as one of the best pieces made by Kemlows as the whole design is produced on the small M55 diecast machine.

*78. **Military Set**
5. 1955,1957. 2/-, 2/6. Uncommon.
Three seated soldiers
(khaki uniforms - in Set 4).
Two seated WRACs (khaki
uniforms)
Seat not included.

79. *Naval Set*   5. 1955,1958. 2/-, 2/6. Uncommon.

Three seated sailors (blue and white). Two seated WRENs (blue and white - in Set 4). Seat not included.

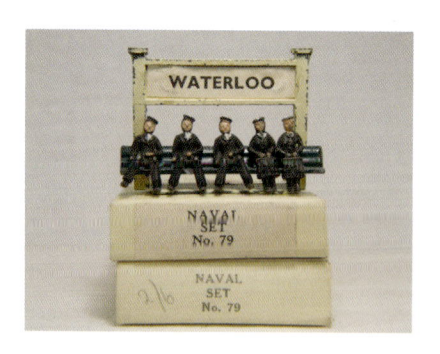

80. *Loading Gauge*   1. 1953,1961. 2/-, 2/6. Common.

Loading gauge (white) on black base plate. This is a redesign of the Don Bowles 'LG' of 1950.

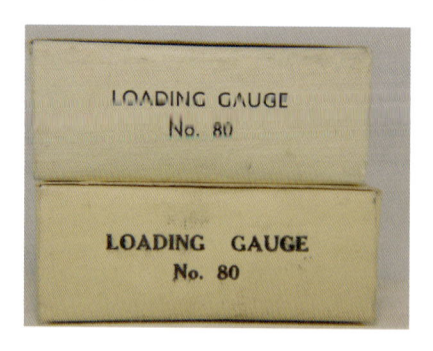

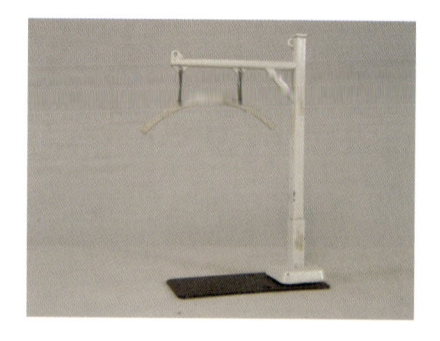

81. *Massey Harris Tractor and Roller*   3. 1956,1961. 2/-. Scarce in box.

Tractor (red, black wheels). Driver (blue or green) seated on peg. Roller (blue or yellow). Roller has 5 wheels, not 6 as in K49. First introduced in 1954 as K49 in the Wee World Series. See also K63 Farm Set.

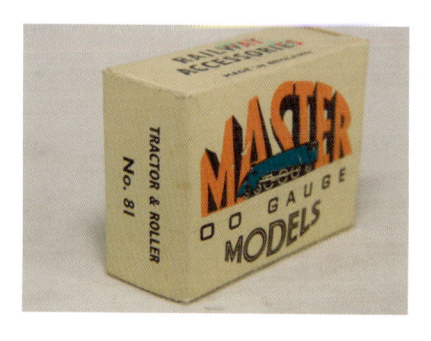

82. Massey Harris Tractor and Rake   3. 1956,1961. 2/-. Scarce in box. Tractor (red, black wheels). Driver (blue or green) seated on peg. Rake (blue) with red wheels. First introduced in 1954 as K50 in the Wee World Series. See also K63 Farm Set.

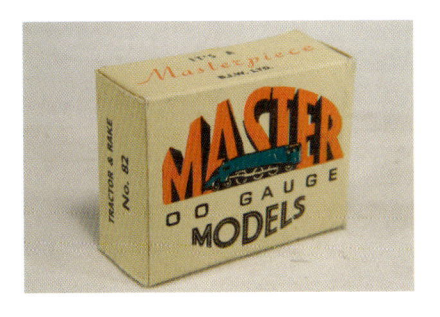

83. Massey Harris Tractor and Farm Cart 5. 1956,1960. 2/-. Scarce in box. Tractor (red, black wheels). Driver (blue or green) seated on peg. Cart (green, black wheels) and two separate raves (grey) that slot into cart ribs. First introduced in 1954 as K47 in the Wee World Series. See also K63 Farm Set.

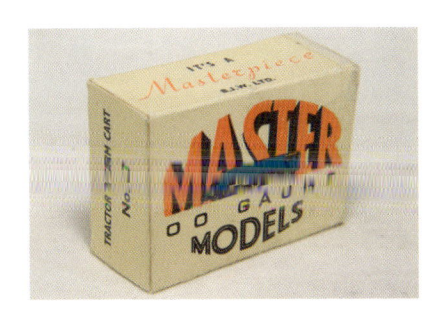

84. Signal Gantry   1. 1956,1962. 7/6, 5/-. Uncommon.
Triple track gantry (matt or gloss black) with painted dummy lights (red, yellow and green). Four holes are drilled through top plate to mount semaphore signals if required.

85. Service Personnel 5. 1957, 1962. 2/6. Uncommon.

Military policeman (khaki uniform). Commando (khaki uniform) with kit bag. Army officer (khaki uniform). WREN (blue and white). Sailor (blue and white) sitting on kit bag.

86. BR Personnel

7. 1957, 1962. 2/6. Uncommon. Driver with lamp (dark blue). Fireman in dungarees (brown). Coach cleaners (blue) on ladder (green or black). Pullman car steward (black and white). Porter (black and khaki) with brush (brown) over his shoulder. Porter and brush are separate pieces. These are all new tooled figures.

87. Double Pump

1, 1956, 1960. 2/-. Quite common. Two '00' gauge petrol pumps (from Set 44) mounted on base plate, separated by motor oil sign "Essolube" or "Shell X 100". All red. Acts as one piece. This is part of the assembly for K16. It was also called K16W in the 1960 Gamages Catalogue.

88. Four Road Side Kiosks 2. 1958,1961. 3/-. Very scarce in box.
RAC box (blue). Enquiries booth (green). Police box (dark blue) and telephone box (red).

These are different castings from the earlier sets. The RAC is a new piece. Note that all the roofs are flat unlike the earlier rounded ones. Some mint sets have been seen with the old kiosks - perhaps using up old stock.

89. Footbridge 1. 1957,1962. 1/6. Quite common.
Footbridge (mid green). Only 6" long, so is difficult to incorporate into a layout. The fences (same design as No 74 railings) are part of the casting.

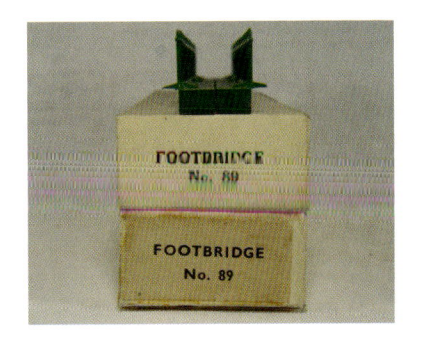

90. Sheep 6. 1960. 1/-. Very scarce in box.
As in Set 11. Britain's Lilliput. Only advertised in 1960 Gamages Catalogue.

91. Not used.

92. Four types of Electric Signals 4. 1957,1959. 5/-. Scarce with box.
Search light junction signal (black) with ladder. Dummy lights. One of Set 53.
Banner signal (black) with ladder. Two round discs (grey, one with red strip and the other green) on horizontal banner. One of Set 54.
Three aspect Colour light signal (black) with ladder. Dummy lights (red, yellow and green) on grey background plate. One of Set 55.
Single aspect searchlight signal (black) with ladder. Dummy light (green) on grey surround. One of Set 56.

93. Not used.

94. Bus and Coach Stops 4. 1958,1961. 2/-. Quite scarce.
Two single flag (red and white) London Transport bus stops (cream). One double flag bus (red and white) and coach (green and white) stop (cream). One coach (green and white) stop (cream) with timetable board.

95. *Assorted Signs* 4. 1958. 2/-. Scarce with box.

Sign board (light blue) with "ROAD UP" printed both sides (K21 of Garage Series). Sign board (light blue) with "NO ENTRY" printed both sides. Sign board (light blue) with "NO PARKING" printed both sides (K20 of Garage Series). Sign board (orange or red oxide) with "OPEN" on one side and "CLOSED" the other (K9 of Garage Series).

96. *Left Luggage Office* 1. 1957, 1962. 5/-. Common.

Left luggage and Parcels Office, double fronted with clock on top centre (grey or green) Sometimes came as double parcels office. Boxes are too short for contents so often creased or damaged.

97. *Oil Storage Tanks* 1. 1957, 1962. 4/6. Scarce in box.

Two tanks (silver) side by side on steel supports. Plastic piping (red or grey) at both ends to represent fuel pipes. The Shell logos are transfers, not paper and are often damaged.

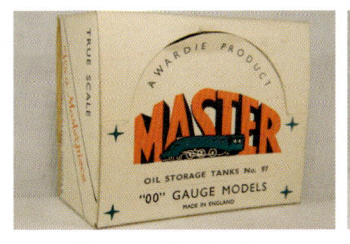

Counter display box

98. Scenic Backgrounds   4. 1961. 8/-. Uncommon.

00. Scenic Backgrounds   4. 1953. 5/6.
Four scenic backgrounds. 20" x 8". In card tube or paper sleeve. First introduced in 1953 without number (see 00).

5800. Single Signal   1. 1961. 1/-. Very scarce in packet.

Paper Advertisements

These were found folded up inside the MasterModel boxes for the numbered sets. Not every set had one and they consequently are not easy to find.
The only ones seen to date are as follows:

Catalogue and Handbook for 1955	3 ⅛″ x 2¾″	Light blue
Catalogue and Handbook for 1956	3 ⅛″ x 2¾″	Mid blue
No 14 W H Smith Bookstall (perhaps the most advertised).	3 ½″ x 2¾″	Beige, cream, light blue and light orange
No's 53, 54, 55 and 56 Signals	3½″ x 2¾″	Pale cream
No 68 Girder Bridge	3½″ x 2¾″	Yellow, pale blue, cream
No 84 Signal Gantry	2 ⅞″ x 2½″	Pink
No 97 Oil Storage Tanks	3½″ x 3″	Cream, pale blue

THE MASTER MODEL RANGE

MasterModel adverts

Five

MasterModel Derivatives

As with any successful range of products there will be repackaging by other companies, both home and abroad as well as companies copying.

In the 1950s BJ Ward did negotiate sole selling rights to other countries. Peter and Joy Cowan had sole selling rights in Canada after Joy had spoken to BJ Ward in London. They sold MasterModels in Canada until the 1970s when most of the stock was returned to the UK for auction on their retirement - I did manage to buy their last items in the 1990s with the Canadian prices still on the boxes.

Polk of Aristocraft did have a large market for MasterModels in the US. He imported the MasterModels from the UK and repackaged them to avoid a tax fee for imports at trade fairs. They were known as the Trackside Range.

If you look at the lists below you can see that in many cases the "old number" is in fact the UK MasterModel number.

It is interesting to see very British items being sold in the US, e.g. the AA Set, Police Set, W H Smith Bookstall and "Waterloo" seat.

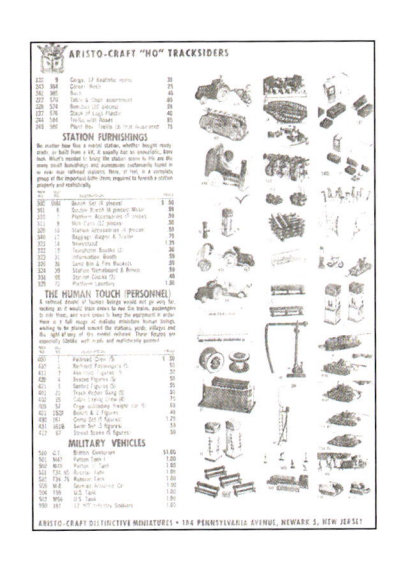

Below is a selection of sets demonstrating Americanisms with truly British items.

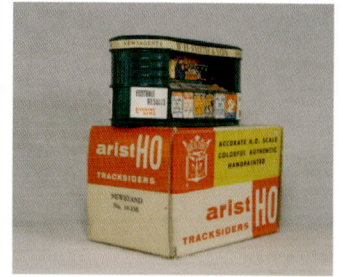

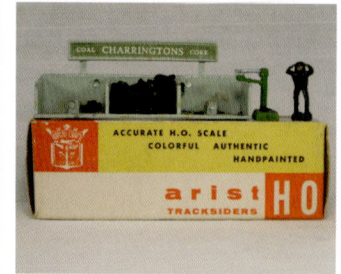

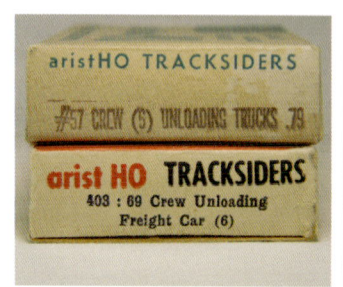

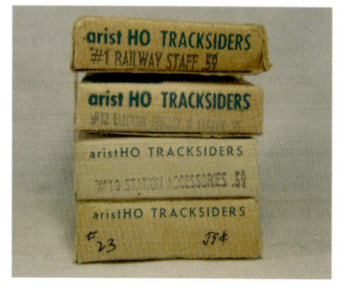

Apart from Canada and the US, MasterModels have been found in numbers in Australia and New Zealand. Imitations have also been produced in Japan by A.H.I. Brand Toys. These are not re-distributions of MasterModels but unmistakeable copies. The bases of the copied figures tend to be larger than the Kemlows castings.

The examples below are ones that have been imported into the UK in the 1960s.

Note a mixture of English and American items

All these are MasterModels copies

All except the cable drum are MasterModel copies

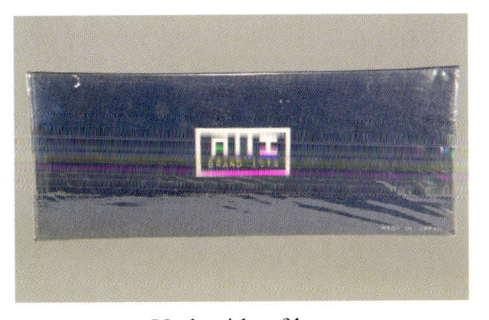

Underside of box

Notice large bases

Underside

128　THE KEMLOW STORY

Close up

Unmistakeable MM with large bases

Re-packaging also occurred in the UK in the 1960s. At a time when sales were waning because of plastics development, I suspect DJ Ward was selling in bulk at discounted prices. If outlets were to dispose of them more effectively, re-packaging would make marketing sense.

The King Charles Sports Centre at 18 King Charles Street, Leeds, sold MasterModels in claret and blue bubble packs. It is not known if they packaged themselves or had it done for them.

MasterModel Derivatives

129

Whilst these are complete MasterModel sets, they do not carry the original set names and numbers.

This advert from Model Railway News in 1965 adequately sums up the situation for diecasting.

These final two pictures show re-packaged MasterModels items from unknown distributors.

Six

The Kemlows 'K' Series

In all of the research I have not come across any hint why the items are prefixed with a K. I can only assume it is to indicate a Kemlows product. Again BJ Ward was the distributor of these items. In the late 1950s "MASTER RANGE" was printed on the end of the yellow illustrated boxes.

The series included garage equipment items, road furniture (approximately '0' scale), Wee World farm items (approximately '00' scale) and various oddities.

The MasterModel Catalogue/Handbooks, advertising flyers and other catalogues described the garage items as "larger than '00' gauge for homemade toy garages".

Items that are OO gauge in the K series are indicated as such after their title.

The series began in 1952 as all diecast and continued well into the 1960s using plastic injection mouldings with the diecast components.

Finally the majority of the items were completely plastic produced by Kemlows.

It will be seen that sometimes the same K number is allocated to the same item which was initially diecast and later plastic e.g. K24 Petrol Pumps and K64 Garage Signs.

In this chapter I will deal with the 1950s diecast 'K series items and deal with the plastic items later.

An initial advertising date will be given as most were available throughout the 1950s. The price given is the initial price.

K9 Open/Closed Sign   1. 1953. 6d. Quite common.

One sign with OPEN one side and CLOSED on reverse. This is the same casting as the one in MasterModels Set 95.

K10 Garage Equipment Set   6. 1952. 5/-. Scarce.

Note that all these items (except the OPEN/CLOSED sign) are available in sets or individually in the 'K' range.

The Open/Closed sign is a different casting from K9 (and so MasterModel Set 95).

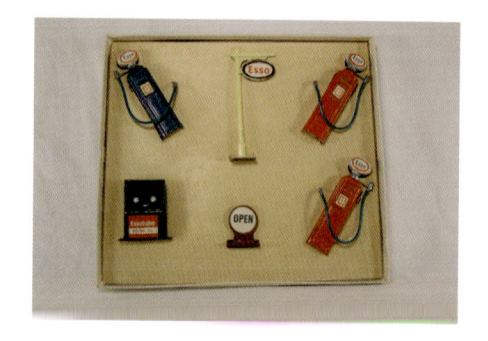

K12 Esso Standard Sign   1. 1952. 8d. Quite common.

Found in white and cream.

K13 Oil Cabinets   1. 1952. 10d. Scarce in box.

Came in Wee World boxes in assorted colours.

K66 was a box of 1 dozen.

K14 Bus Stop　　　　　　1. 1955. 6d. Quite common.
As found in MasterModel No 94 Set.

K15 Coach Stop　　　　　1. 1955. 6d. Quite common.
As found in MasterModel No 94 Set.

K16 Filling Station ("00")　3. 1953. 2/6. Not common.
Two loose '00' pumps (MasterModels Set No 44) slotted onto filling station assembly. Only red and blue pumps seen in boxes, but green were available.

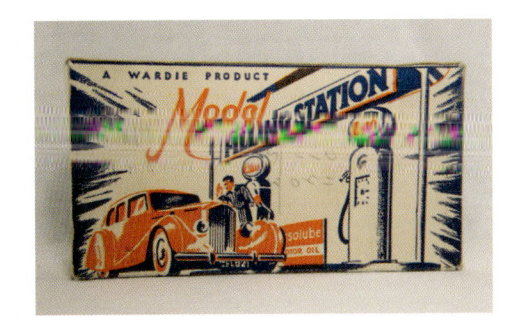

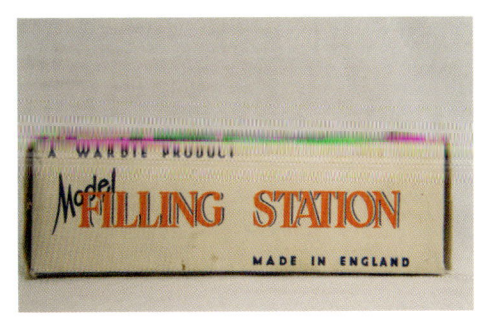

K16 Filling Station ("00")　1. 1953. 2/6. Not common.

Pair of '00' pumps fixed to their own base (MasterModel Set No87) mounted onto filling station assembly.

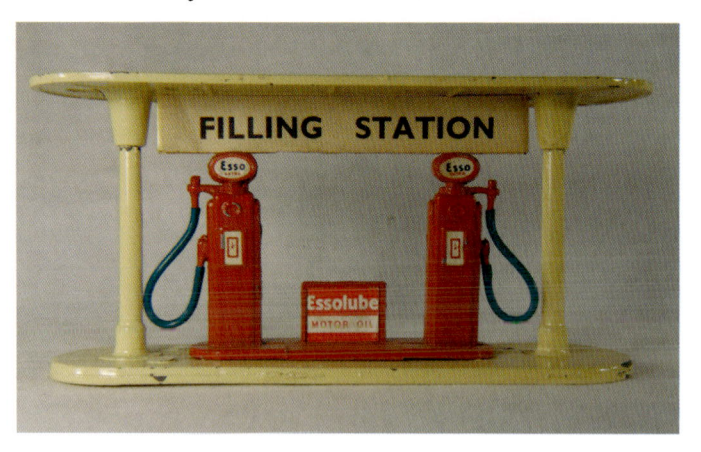

K16 Filling Station ("00") 1. Scarce.

A completely different casting from the previous examples. Whilst the "00" pumps are mounted on their own base as previously, the pumps are further apart. The red casting is all one unit.

K16W Filling Station without canopy ("00") 1. 1959. 2/3. Quite common.

This is the MasterModel No87 Double Pump set. The coding is unusual, so suggests it is not BJ Ward's coding. This code K16W only appeared in the 1960 Gamages catalogue.

K16W Filling Station without canopy   1. 1959. 2/3. Scarce.

As above, but the MasterModel Double Pump Set No 87 is fixed to a kidney shaped base.

Not advertised.

K17 Garage Personnel   9. 1955. 3/6. Scarce.

This set is also available in a smaller box, less the air pump, as K60.

These pieces are usually found in a fatigued condition, suffering from intergranular corrosion.

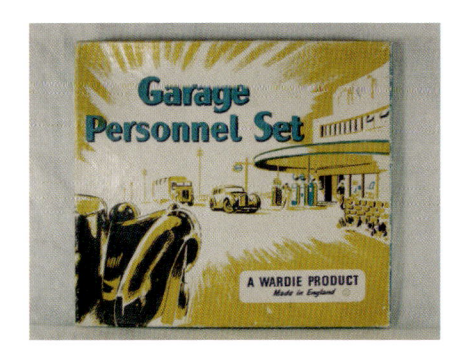

K18 Service Station   6. 1955. 2/11. Rare with box.

This is a new casting not utilising the '00' MasterModel pumps. All five items fit onto the kidney shaped base.

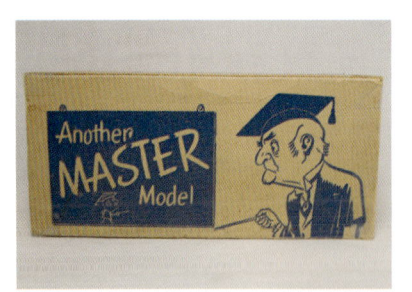

K18 Service Station   6. 1955. 2/11. Scarce.

As above but different pump globes and box.

These castings were susceptible to damage as the pump levers often broke off. Consequently you will have one of three variations. The first one is complete as in the picture. The second, the levers have broken off after leaving the factory and so have bare metal at the joints. The third is where the levers broke off at the foundry and the broken joints were later painted when being sprayed.

K18 Service Station   4. Scarce.

Pumps on a kidney base. Not really a Service Station but a Filling Station. No literature has been found to clarify the K18 reference to this example.

K18 Service Station   3. 1960s. Scarce.

Pumps on base. These pumps are a later casting. Not really a Service Station but a Filling Station. No literature has been found to clarify the K18 reference to this example.

K19 Petrol Pumps   1. 1957. 1/1.

One of Shell, Esso, BP, Fina, Regent and Mobilgas.

Only one reference to this earlier casting whose design does not appear later. These pumps have cast globes. The boxed set contains only Shell pumps even though it says assorted brands on the box. I consider the contents correct as this set has been seen numerous times. It is perhaps a counter box to sell these pumps individually.

Individually boxed

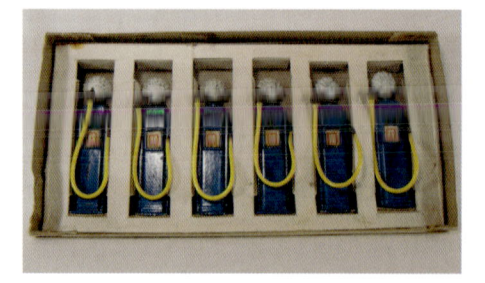

Counter box

K20 No Parking Sign   1. 1952. 6d. Not common.
This is the same casting as the one in MasterModels Set 95.

K21 Road Up Sign   1. 1952. 6d. Not common.

This is the same casting as the one in MasterModels Set 95.

K23 Petrol Pumps   1. 1958. 1/4. Rare in boxes.

One of Shell, Esso, BP, Fina, National Benzole and Mobilgas. Diffcrent improved design to K19. With plastic globes.

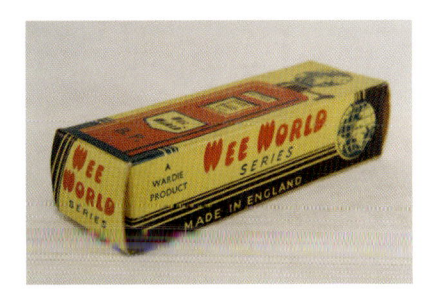

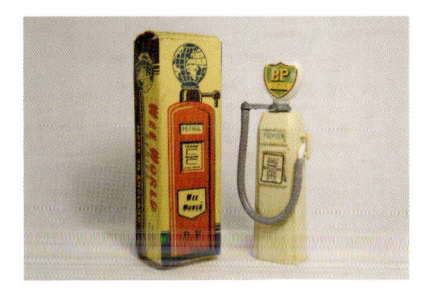

K24 Petrol Pumps   6. 1958. 7/11.

A box of the six different pumps from K23.

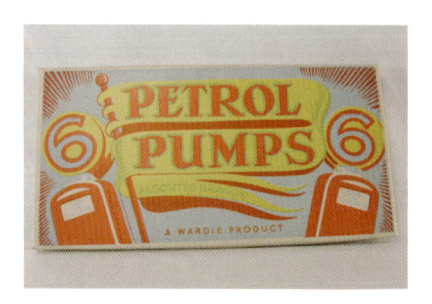

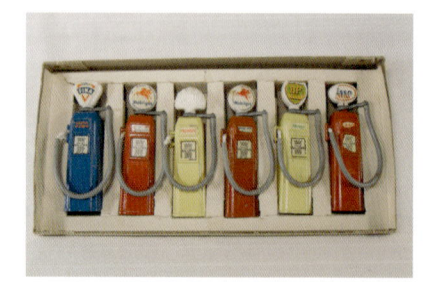

K24 Petrol Pumps   6. 1963. Sold at 1/6 each, as well as boxes. Not common.

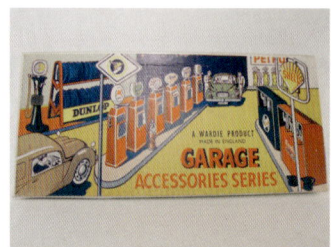

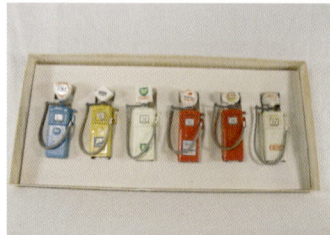

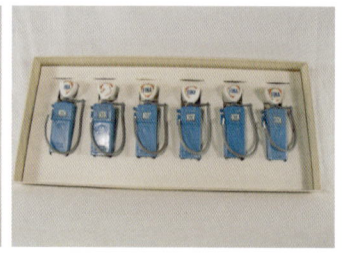

This is a different design from the previous two designs.

The following were sold individually in stapled packets. All are scarce.

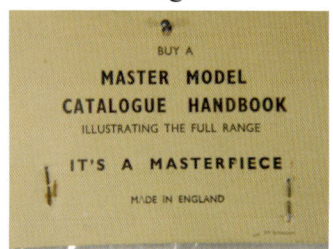

Reverse of stapled packet

The Kemlows 'K' Series

Wee World Farm Series. Sold as 00 gauge
See also MasterModels Sets 81, 82 and 83.

K47 Massey-Harris Tractor and Farm Cart   5. 1954. 2/-. Not common.
This became MasterModel No 83 in 1957.

Tractor (red, black wheels). Driver (silver) seated on peg. Cart (mid or lime green) and two raves (yellow or grey) that slot into cart ribs.

See K 63 Farm Set.

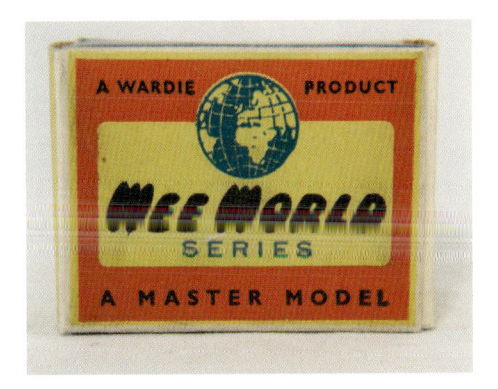

Mid green cart, grey raves   Lime green cart, yellow raves

Small, long box, very tight fit so box usually damaged. Cart always appears to be lime green

K48 Cement Mixer   1954. 1/6. Not common.

This appears to be larger than '00' gauge. Note the different components variations of colour, and wheel types.

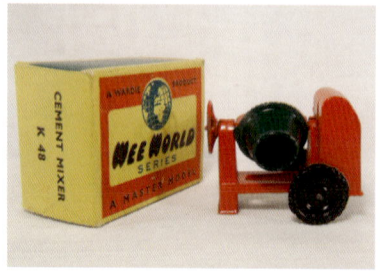

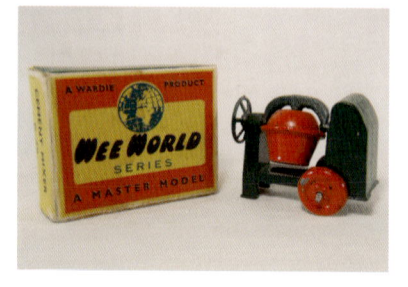

K49 Massey-Harris Tractor and Roller   3. 1954. 2/-. Not common.

This became MasterModel No 81 in 1957.

Tractor (red, black wheels). Driver (black or silver) seated on peg. Roller (mid blue or light blue or yellow or green) has 6 wheels. MasterModels No 81 roller has 5 wheels.

A variety of boxes were used with this model. The cement mixer box (K48) with labels on the end was often used when boxes were short. See K 63 Farm Set.

The Kemlows 'K' Series   143

Cement mixer box with unusual labels

Cement mixer box with usual label

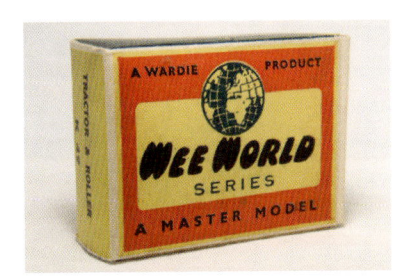

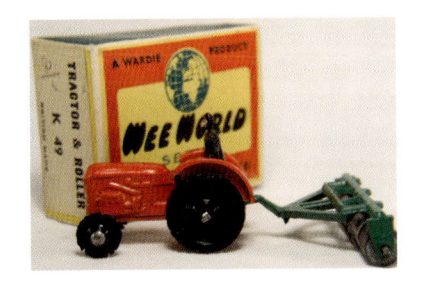

24 ex-shop stock

K50 Massey-Harris Tractor and Rake   3. 1954. 2/-. Not common.
This became MasterModel No 82 in 1957.
Tractor (red, black wheels). Driver (black or green) seated on peg. Rake (dark blue or light blue with red wheels).
Note the variations of boxes and wheels.
See K 63 Farm Set.

Cement mixer box with label

Factory error. Wrong wheels fitted to front

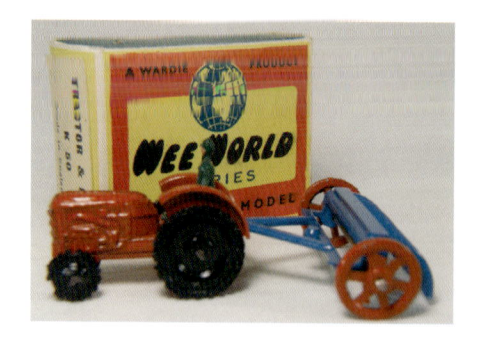

Unusual grey metal wheels

K51 Fire Engine   1. 1954. 1/6. Rare.
A red fire engine with silver ladder. Supposedly 00 but smaller. Of the ones seen so far the castings have been poor. A rare item.

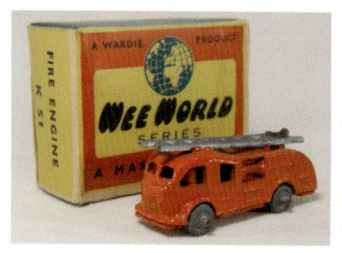

K54 Car Ramps   12. 1956. Sold separately for 1/3 to 1/9.

Rare in counter box.

Advertised as "matchbox size" and sold individually from a counter box containing 12.

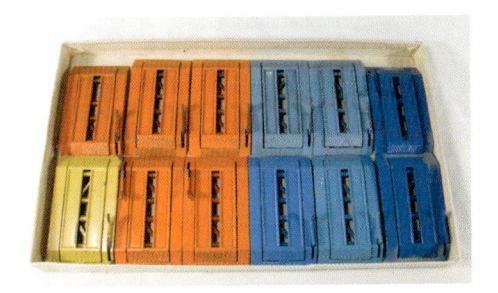

K56 4 Sheep in Pen   5. 1956. 2/6. Very rare.

Four grey Britain's Lilliput sheep on a wooden grey base pen. Enclosure is metal fencing (fawn) with a gate.

Note that MasterModel No 11 is an identical set, but usually with green fences. This set is extremely rare and so suspect that BJ Ward had a few boxed up as K56 then reverted to his more usual MasterModel numbering.

K57 Windmill   1. 1958. 1/6. Not common.

Rather an odd item for Kemlows to produce, or indeed for anyone. First produced and sold in 1949 for BJ Ward to release almost 10 years later in the K-Series. Concerned about the Kemlows name on the back of one sail, the name was chiselled off the die. It is an early example if it escaped this fate.

It stands only 3 $5/8$" tall with the sail extended vertically.

THE KEMLOW STORY

"Kemlows" chiselled off the die

"Kemlows" intact

K58 Tyre Rack   1. 1958. 2/11. Not common. Counter box of 12. Very rare.

Most common boxed individually.

Garage tyre rack (red) to hold 12 small and 12 large tyres (rubber - supplied by Collis who Kemlows now owned). Similar to Dinky, but the Kemlows yellow label has "DUNLOP" printed vertically rather than leaning forward. The castings are also different in that the end supports of the Kemlows are bent at a sharp 100° rather than an arc as in the Dinky.

First use in the K Series of the words "Master Range" and "A Master True Scale Model".

The Kemlows 'K' Series   147

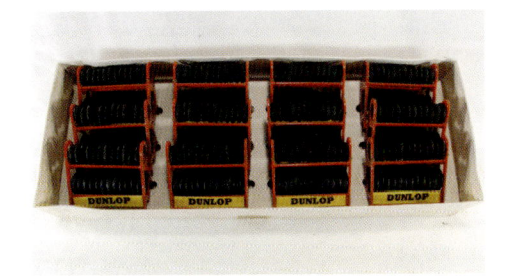

A counter box containing a dozen racks

K58 Tyre Rack   25. 1960s. Not common in box.

A later design where the red side pieces and central tyre supports are plastic. The tyres are also plastic rather than rubber.

Mainly plastic tyres rack

K58 Private Garage   1957. 1/6. Not common.

This is an attractive delicate all metal piece. Be careful on opening the doors as any metal fatigue will result in the hinges snapping off.

A range of colours have been seen, but the grey with green doors is most common.

Different print format on box end has been found.

Most common colours

Never been opened

K60 Garage Set   8. 1958. 2/5, 2/6. Rare.

A compressor (red) with air line (yellow) being operated by mechanic (white overalls/coat and black cap). Mechanic (brown overalls and beige shirt) holding tyre (all one piece) whilst kneeling mechanic (brown) helps. Car sprayer (brown, black cap) and mask (silver) with spray gun (silver). Finisher (black trousers, white cap and coat) with chamois. Trolley jack (red) with mechanic (black trousers, blue shirt) lying beside. These pieces are usually found in a fatigued condition, suffering from intergranular corrosion. A rare set in either a box or a packet.

K61 Garage Walls   1958. 1/6 each. Scarce.

Sold as Wee World (larger than 00) individually from a counter box. The counter box shown is a rare item.

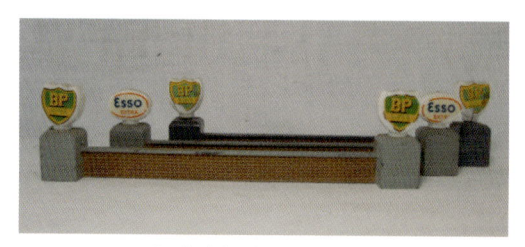

Individual examples

Rare counter box

K63 Farm Implements   7. 1956. 2/6, 3/11. Rare.

Sold as Wee World ('00'). This is the combined set of K47 (Farm Cart), K49 (Roller) and K50 (Rake).

Sets come with no particular combination of colours. The box is a flip-up counter box.

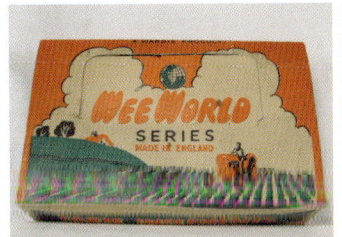

This particular set was found in New Zealand

K64 Garage Signs   6. 1958. 1/- each (Set 5/11). Rare in box.

Sold as Wee World. Came as any combination of Mobilgas, BP, Fina, Shell, Esso and National Benzole. All metal.

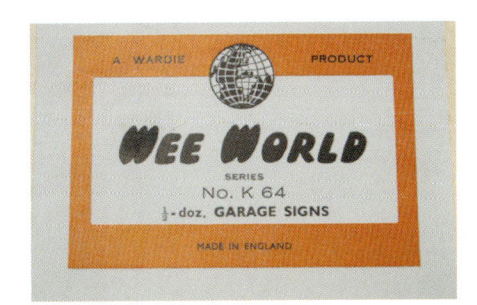

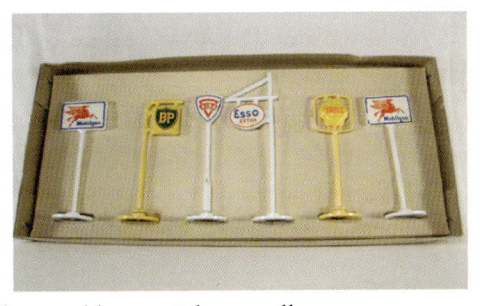

Counter box, but would have been sold separately as well

K64 Garage Signs   6. 1963. 9d each. Scarce.

Came as any combination of Mobilgas, BP, Fina, Shell, Esso and National Benzole. All plastic injection. Similar are found in the Build-a-Garage series later.

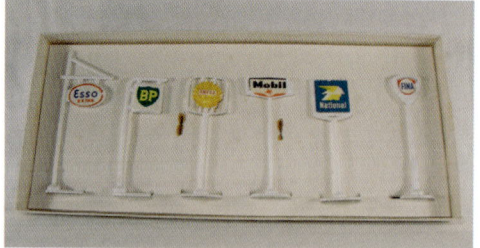

Counter box but would have been sold separately as well

K65 Air Pumps   12. 1958. 1/2 each. Rare in box.

Twelve air pumps in shop counter box, sold individually (green or blue or beige). Cast collars with yellow air hoses and white triggers. Plastic globes.

K66 Oil Cabinets   12. 1958. 1/3 each. Rare in box.

Twelve all metal oil cabinets (red or green or beige) in counter box. These were also sold individually boxed (K13).
Cabinets have sliding shutters and three dummy pumps.

K67 Garage Equipment Set 6. 1959. 8/11. Scarce.

A set comprising of items from other sets. Two pumps (K24), two garage signs (K64 metal), one oil cabinet (K13 or K66) and one tyre rack (K58).

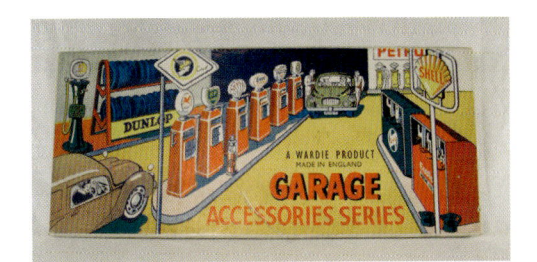

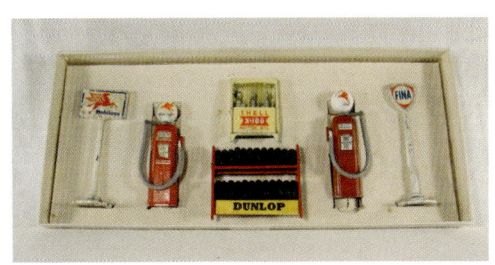

Earlier K24 pumps

K67 Garage Equipment Set 6. 1963. 9/3. Scarce.

A set similar to the one above but the later cast K24 pumps.

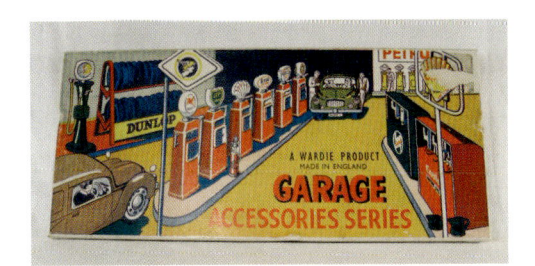

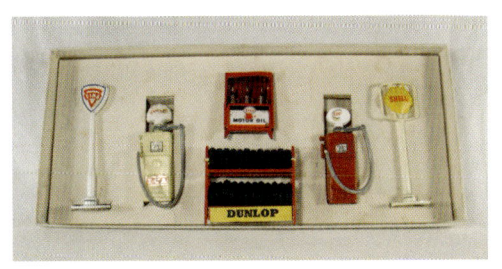

K68 Filling Station 1. 1964. 3/6. Scarce in box.

All diecast filling station fixed as one piece. The later K24 diecast pumps are used and crimped into the base. The central post supports two fluorescent light tubes.

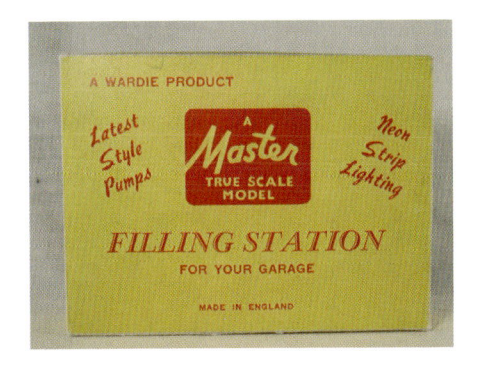

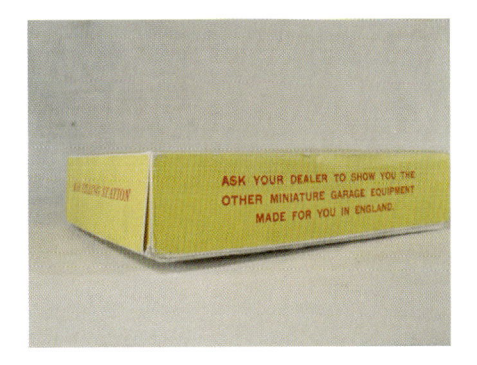

K69 Car Ramp   1. 1964. 2/6. Scarce in box.

A larger version of K54 advertised as suitable for Dinky Toys and coming in a vermilion colour. The only markings are "MADE IN ENGLAND", typical of Kemlows.

If there is a patent number or any other markings, it isn't a Kemlows K69. DCMT and Crescent look very similar.

K70 Garage Forecourt   6. 1966.

K71 Oil Cabinets   12.

A mention here of the last two items in the K-Series, both of these are plastic. See the Chapter on Kemlows Plastic.

K90 Garage Posters

Printed by JNT Model Products. Packets of posters stapled to a card. The card shows K90 in the corner. This could be another item bought in by BJ Ward in the 1960s or just a pure coincidence of labelling.

The following later items are the only known items to appear in the Kemlows 'K' Series that were either part or all plastic. See the chapter on Kemlows Plastics.

K24 6 Assorted Pumps (Part plastic and part cast).

K64 Petrol Signs (All plastic).

K67 Garage Equipment (mainly plastic).

K70 Filling Station (Mainly plastic).

K71 12 Oil Cabinets (All plastic).

Seven

Other Kemlows diecast Products

Pickfords Guy Pantechnicon Van

This was produced in the 1950s and close to '00' gauge. No ledger reference is made of this so is post 1952. As this was made solely for Pickfords no advertising material exists either. This is a one off item.

Stephen Lowe considers the Pickfords van to be one of the best items Kemlows made. It seems to be a tie between this and the MasterModels Girder Bridge.

It was made exclusively for Pickfords to be given to customers as a thank-you for their custom. It is not known why this wonderful model was not further developed but Kemlows was now extremely busy with BJ Ward orders.

The van was wrapped in brown paper.

Rocket Launcher (late 1950s).

This was designed by Stephen Lowe when he was approximately 8-10 years old. His father asked for ideas and Stephen came up with the launcher.
The casting is one piece and the legs are fixed, the feet being at distances 3 ¾" x 3 ¼". The central tube is spring loaded with a lever pulling down the central rod and the lever then rotated to hold it. The rocket is launched by flicking the lever and so releasing the spring. The original rocket was diecast, but as it only reached a height of about six inches, Collis made a plastic one which reached about six feet. Stephen has an original cast rocket which will be extremely rare.

Road Roller (1950s).

The '00' gauge road roller is not always recognised as being Kemlows as other similar models were available. It fits in nicely with the release of the Sentry Box Series.

The Sentry Box Series

This small collection of wonderful matchbox size military vehicles was produced as direct competition to the more famous Matchbox products.
Lilian Lowe (wife of the founder of Kemlows, William Lowe) says that this was a suggestion of hers to William as the Matchbox series was highly successful. She also came up with the sentry box idea to market them.
Period of production is difficult to pin down as ledgers do not exist for the late 1950s, but it must have been about this period to be competing with Matchbox. The demise of Kemlows military model production came in the early 1960s as a result of the campaigns against military toys headed by people like Mary Whitehouse.
This brief period of production explains why those items are not easy to find.
I think the boxes are perhaps the best and most distinguishing feature of this product.
Again, there are no marks on the items to say they are Kemlows except for the usual die stamp "MADE IN ENGLAND". This is almost a signature in itself for Kemlows products. Charlie Kempster was in charge of sales and distribution and never really pushed the Kemlows name with any of their products.
With the demise of military models in Britain in the 1960s, the Sentry Box dies were sold to Gamda in Israel, who then produced models. The Centurion Tank and Tank Transporter were advertised by Gamda.

The 3-Ton Bedford Lorry

Don't forget, this is small, only 2 ¼" long. One piece casting.

Base of box

The 3-Ton Bedford Lorry Towing 25 pdr

Bedford 2 ¼″ long. 25 pdr 2 ⅜″ long.

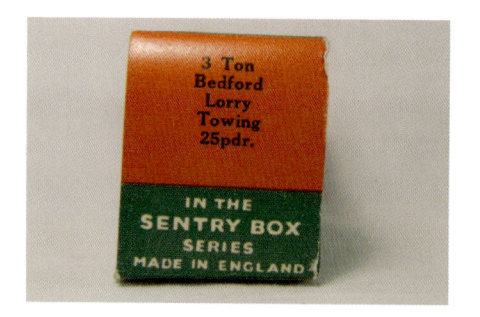

Base of box

Tank Transporter

A long piece that comes as one unit. Quite useful when trying to keep an Antar together. Length 6 ½". The tank does not come with this item - it wouldn't fit in the box as well. Similar, but different from the Matchbox version, having more angular features.

A scarce item with a box.

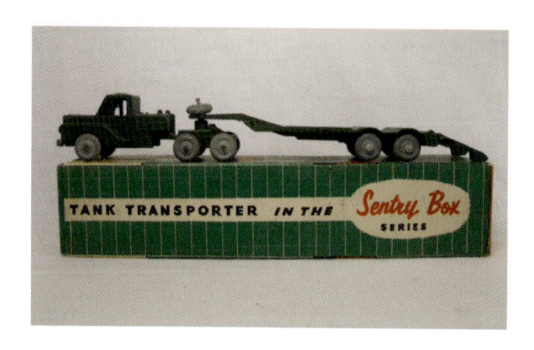

Armoured Vehicle

This armoured car is 2 ¼" long with a rotating turret.

Base of box

Armoured Vehicle with Limber and Gun

This is a rare item that I've not seen in a box. It consists of a modified Armoured Vehicle (towing hook added), a Limber and a modified 25 pdr gun (towing eye and box added).

Tank

This is a Centurion tank 2 ¼" long with a rotating turret. The wheels and track seen in the pictures are part of the casting. Four hidden wheels underneath give its movement.

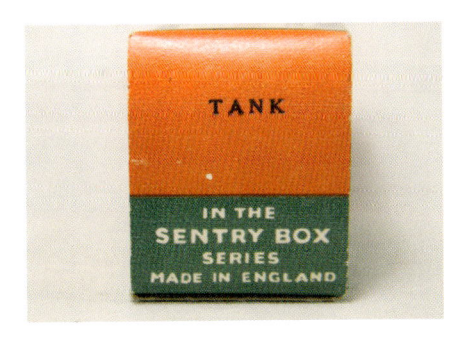

Base of box    Visible wheels and track are part of cast

The Military Master Range   Scale 1:60

At approximately the same time as Kemlows were producing their Sentry Box Series military items, they were also producing their larger Military Master Range. Again mainly distributed through Woolworths, this series had little advertising literature, so dates are difficult to pin down. Some of BJ Ward's flyers do have dates of 1958 for these items though.

The Dedford castings became the basis of the Autamec range in the late 1950s (see later). In 1956 the Artillery Set was sold by Strome & Co who were wholesalers at that time.

The Range suffered the same fate as the Sentry Box Series in the early 1960s. Again, no Kemlows markings are found on this range, except for the usual "MADE IN ENGLAND" die stamp.

M9 Quad, Limber and Field Gun (Military Set)   1958.   7/6.

A beautiful set, overall length of 9 ¼". This is rare in the box. All items were available individually (M10, M11 and M12). See each for details.

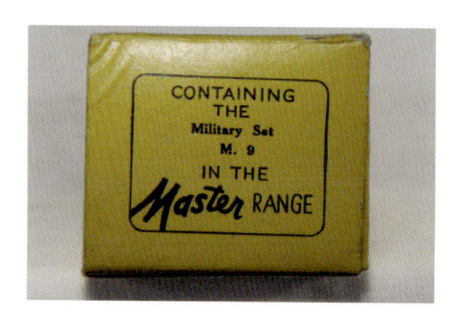

OTHER KEMLOWS DIECAST PRODUCTS 161

Quad

Limber

25 pdr Field Gun

M10 25 pounder Field Gun 1958. 2/-.

Overall length is 4". A working model with spring loaded barrel and draw lever (these are now usually rusty and need careful lubrication). No markings.

Usual box

Unusual colourful box - perhaps for Woolworths stores

M11 Gun Limber   1958. 2/-.

Overall length is 2 ³⁄₈″. The limber opens to show 6 shells for the gun to fire. Only marking is "MADE IN ENGLAND" die stamp in a circle on base.

M12 Armoured Quad   1958. 3/6.

Overall length 3 ¼". Only marking is "MADE IN ENGLAND" die stamped on base.

Artillery Set

Overall length 10 ½". The set consists of the 3-Ton Bedford (see below) with the Limber (M11 above) and 25 pounder Field Gun (M10 above).

The set is similar to the Quad, Limber and Field Gun set M9 with the Bedford replacing the Quad.

The picture box again suggests packaged for Woolworths distribution. More common than the M9 set, but still very difficult to find.

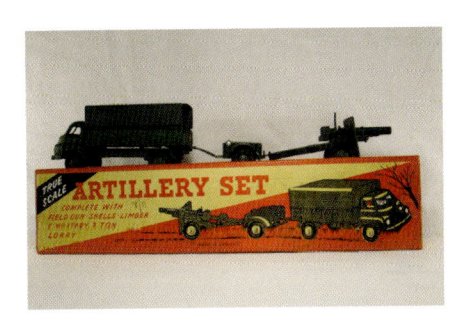

3-Ton Bedford

Overall length 4 ½". Much has been written about the Kemlows 3-Ton Bedford being a good copy of the 1954 Dinky Toys No 621 3-Ton Army Wagon. Only by turning them over and seeing the Dinky Toy stamp or Kemlows "MADE IN ENGLAND" stamp tells you. The Kemlows version doesn't have a driver either.

Kemlows　　　　　　　　　　　Dinky Toys

Automec

After numerous runs of the Bedford, two brothers in Lincoln negotiated with Kemlows to have this Bedford cast for them so that they could produce variations of the Bedford.

They became the main selling item of Basil and Stan Clark's Automec Company in Lincoln. Kemlows produced the main castings and Automec provided (bought in) the tin tilts. They proceeded in modifications and respraying to provide different looking vehicles. They even drilled out the rivets to take them apart so as to provide kits. Some ended up looking little like the originals.

A full illustrated history of this company is in print in an easy to read booklet form.[3]

These are some slight modifications (spraying and tilts)

Armoured Car

Overall length 2 ¾". This item has no serial number but fits into the Master Range. Again a faithful copy of the Dinky Toys No 670 Daimler (1954), only the base stamps distinguishing them.

OTHER KEMLOWS DIECAST PRODUCTS   165

Base stamp

The sales flyer below shows that some of these items make it to the American market. With the absence of BJ Ward marketing, it can only be guess work without records.

Military pieces of Fred Bronner, New York

Eight

Kemlows Plastics

In Chapter One the move into plastics is described. It was a natural move as diecasting was now being rapidly replaced in toy manufacturing by plastic mould injection. As luck would have it Collis Plastics factory was next door but one to Kemlows new factory at Potters Bar in 1958.

Whilst Collis Plastics main business was industrial plastic moulding they did provide Kemlows with plastic parts e.g. petrol pump globes and tyres. After Kemlows acquisition of Collis, industrial moulding continued and plastic toy moulding grew.

The early items were picked up and distributed by BJ Ward as he moved into plastic model garage equipment. In the 1960s BJ Ward was struggling to sell the traditional diecasting and moved into other areas. Being a true entrepreneur he would sell anything. His 1960s catalogues show his move away from MasterModels and into other areas.

Kemlows plastic garage items were distributed by BJ Ward, but soon afterwards the Lowe brothers took charge. Distribution was also through Barton Toys of Croydon.

The object of this chapter is to give examples of the final toy making products made by Kemlows utilising plastics before moving over to industrial moulding completely.

MasterModel

The following examples are all plastic and distributed by BJ Ward. These are identical (except for the larger bases) to the diecast versions by Kemlows.

All three from the original early Set 1 Railway Staff

All three from original later Set 1 Railway Staff

The next example is the all plastic Set No 1 Railway Staff in a stapled packet. These examples have turned up in reasonable quantities - but still rare.
It consists of the three examples shown above from the later Set 1, plus three further items; a man pushing sack trolley (Original Set 1), sack trolley (Similar to original Set 1, but very large parcel on forks), and a man leaning on tall milk churn. Neither moulds seen before.

Second and third additional items as listed above

Complete set

A BJ Ward MasterModel stapled packet

This is where speculation creeps in.

Were all the items made by Kemlows (ex-Collis) Plastics and again distributed by BJ Ward or some made by Kemlows and others by Merit (say), or all made by Merit (say) using their own plastic injections and old Kemlows?

To add to the confusion, Stephen Lowe has a packet of Kemlows items, with a Merit label inside.

Below is another plastic set which is identical to the Kemlows MasterModel diecast set, but did someone else make it with copy moulds, or are they genuine Kemlows plastic mouldings?

Plastic Set No 57

Set 57 contents

The following items are again all plastic but from Kemlows diecast MasterModel range.

This further example is also from the diecast MasterModel range. This is identical to No 40 Permanent Way Cabin less the barrel, BUT there is a mark on the plastic base where the barrel would have slotted i.e. the identical mould. This should, of course, be probably made by Kemlows.

Plastic Permanent Way Cabin

Plastic and diecast side by side

Kemlows "Build a Garage" Series

These have been mentioned in the K Series chapter and are the natural development of the K Series into plastics during the 1960s.

These were made by Kemlows using the "Master Model" name on the box. BJ Ward's name is not found on the boxes. This is the first time on a new Kemlows item since the early 1950s (excluding Woolworths Master and Sentry Box Series) that BJ Ward's name was not put on the packaging. Kemlows moved on and used A Barton & Co (Toys) of Croydon to distribute their new plastic range.

This relationship became so successful that Kemlows eventually sold their plastics toy division to Barton in the 1980s.

K24 Assorted Petrol Pumps Uncommon.

Six assorted petrol pumps, part plastic and part diecast. A box has also been seen with Fina pumps in as well. Substantial sturdy pieces.

K64 Petrol Signs (12)   Uncommon.

These are a plastic version of the all cast K64 sets from 1958.

K64 Petrol Signs (6)   1963. 9d each. Scarce.

An all plastic set that strictly doesn't belong in this series but in the K Series (see the K Series chapter). The box is an old 1950s Wee World box labelled K64.

K67 Garage Equipment   Uncommon.

Mainly plastic set. Some diecasting in pumps and tyre rack stretchers.

K70 Filling Station   Uncommon.

A new design filling station and new design tyre rack (all plastic).

K71 Oil Cabinets (12)   Rare.

A trade box of 12 all plastic oil cabinets.

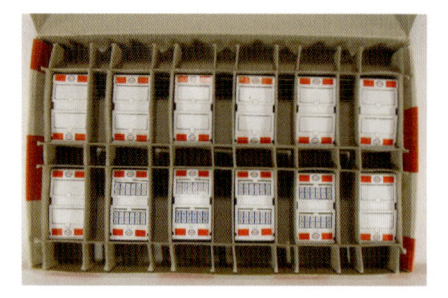

The following four sets are examples of the smaller items in more affordable bubble packs. The packaging is still Build-a-Garage series with Master Model also present. Uncommon.

Plastic and cast petrol pump. New design canopy

Three plastic and cast petrol pumps

Three plastic Garage Signs

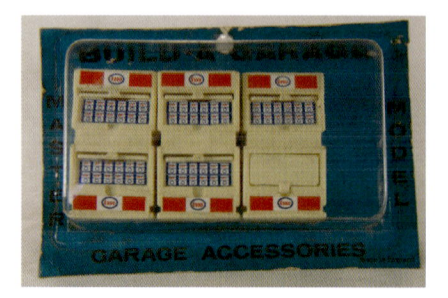

All plastic Oil Cabinets

The words Build a Garage and Master Model are now dropped from the packaging, but the backing card pictures are the same. AB Barton appears for the first time in the top left corner. The address appears in the bottom right corner as A BARTON & CO (TOYS) LTD, Vulcan Way, New Addington, Croydon, CR9 OBU.

All items are in previous sets except the car ramp and road side signs (never seen before). The following three examples appear in small bubble window packs.

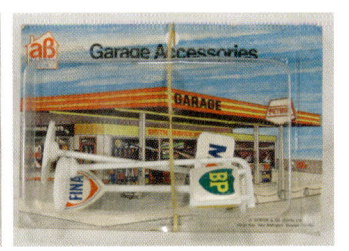

The following examples, still provided by Kemlows, but appearing in Barton's Motoplay series. The packaging loses any traces of the previous MasterModel connections.

This Service Centre is in fact a repackaging of the Kemlows K Series No K70 Filling Station and its MasterModel wording.

The Car Wash is a really tidy example and difficult to come by. Made in approximately 1970 it utilises the best of all design and production features.

The next example is one which Stephen Lowe designed and produced in the early 1970s when trying to regenerate the company away from model railway accessories and toward the more popular car oriented market. This was a set of traffic lights with a rotating cylinder operated from on top. On rotating you would pass through all the different colour sequences of the lights.

KEMLOWS PLASTICS   175

These traffic lights were perhaps the last toy item Kemlows produced. The final story is a good place to finish because it demonstrates something we may forget when thinking of toy manufacturing in the 1940s - 1970s. That is the human aspect. We are not just talking of factories churning out items to be sold, but the families and friends trying to come up with ideas to serve a market, as well as making a living.

The Kemlows toy found guilty

The two pictures below are of a Kemlows item distributed by Barton.

An innocent looking table and four chairs, but the cast table and seat legs caused the problem.

When transporting these metal items by lorry, several boxes full fell out of the back of the lorry. On impact on the road behind, the contents were strewn across the road - an instant "stinger".

This resulted in following cars tyres being punctured. The arm of the law soon extended to Kemlows doors as this was quite a serious situation.

The police reached a decision to try to appease the deflated drivers. Kemlows agreed that any driver having to have repairs to their tyres would have their expenses met by Kemlows.

Quite an expensive table and four chairs in the end.

APPENDIX

Early Kemlows non-toy items

7th January, 1949:   Coffin Rings. 3/- per dozen. 3,000 sold.

22nd February, 1949 - 1st March 1952:

        Buttons. 9/- to 12/- per gross. 108,914 sold.

Two main customers only. These were buttons for uniforms.

23rd March 1949 - 1st May 1950:

        Letters for War Graves Commission. 51,820 sold to Griggs & Son.

January 1951:   Glass cutter handles, 2,500 sold.

        Glass cutters, 15,300 sold.

All sold to one supplier.

1st August 1951:   Guinea Pig Club badges. 258 sold.

The Guinea Pig Club was the unique club of RAF crew who were burned in the Second World War and required pioneering plastic surgery. Based in East Grinstead.

BIBLIOGRAPHY

1) Hailey Models   P & J Brookes   October 2006
2) Gilco Traffic Signs   P & J Brookes   2005
3) Automec   P & J Brookes   2005

KEMLOWS BEST

Kemlows two most innovative products according to Stephen Lowe of Kemlows.

180

PERHAPS THE RAREST MASTERMODELS

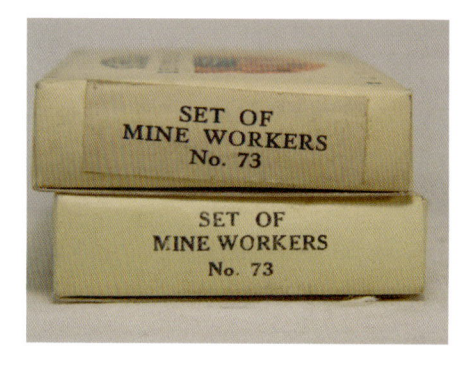